Pilgr to Lourdes

Sally Martin and her husband John have lived in Hampshire since they married in 1966. They have four sons – all of whom went to Ampleforth College, the Benedictine school in North Yorkshire, which runs an annual pilgrimage to Lourdes. It is from here that the family's interest in Lourdes developed when their eldest son joined an Ampleforth pilgrimage in 1985. Since then, the Martins have made a total of 76 visits to Lourdes.

Also available in the *Every Pilgrim's Guide* series:

Every Pilgrim's Guide to Assisi
Judith Dean

*Every Pilgrim's Guide to
Celtic Britain and Ireland*
Andrew Jones

Every Pilgrim's Guide to England's Holy Places
Michael Counsell

Every Pilgrim's Guide to the Holy Land
Norman Wareham and Jill Gill

*Every Pilgrim's Guide to the Journeys of
the Apostles*
Michael Counsell

Every Pilgrim's Guide to Oberammergau
Michael Counsell

www.scm-canterburypress.co.uk

Every Pilgrim's Guide to Lourdes

SALLY MARTIN

CANTERBURY
PRESS
Norwich

First published in 2005 by the Canterbury Press Norwich
(a publishing imprint of Hymns Ancient & Modern Limited,
a registered charity)
St Mary's Works, St Mary's Plain,
Norwich, Norfolk, NR3 3BH

www.scm-canterburypress.co.uk

The words of the 'Stabat Mater' (the Latin hymn on the
suffering of the Virgin Mary at the Crucifixion), ascribed to
Jacopone da Todi (d. 1306) and translated by E. Caswall (1814–78),
are taken from *Hymns Old and New, 1996*.

Scripture readings are taken from the Jerusalem Bible published and
copyright © 1966, 1967 and 1968 by Darton, Longman & Todd Limited
and Doubleday & Co. Inc.

Scripture readings are taken from the Catholic Truth Society, Revised
Standard Version of the Bible, Catholic Edition, published by Thomas
Nelson & Sons Ltd for the Incorporated Catholic Truth Society, London,
copyright © 1966 by the Division of Christian Education of the National
Council of the Churches of Christ in the USA. All rights reserved.

British Library Cataloguing in Publication data

A catalogue record for this book is available
from the British Library

ISBN 1-85311-627-0

Maps by John Flower
Typeset by Rowland Phototypesetting Ltd
Bury St Edmunds, Suffolk
Printed and bound by
Bookmarque, Croydon, Surrey

Contents

Preface

My first visits to Lourdes were during 1959–62, when as a young man I worked as a Brancardier (stretcher-bearer). That experience encouraged my monastic vocation. For five years from 1992 I returned as a priest helping the permanent chaplains working for both the Day Pilgrim Service and in the Chapel of Reconciliation. In 1997 I was elected Abbot of Ampleforth Abbey, and have since led the annual pilgrimage from the Abbey.

Lourdes offers something for everyone. Young or old, sick or healthy, fervent believer or sceptical agnostic. It attracts some six million pilgrims a year from all over the globe, though Europe produces the largest numbers. Most are Roman Catholic, but some are from other Christian denominations and even other faiths. All see Lourdes as a holy place, blessed with the presence of God.

Like many centres of pilgrimage, Lourdes is full of attractions. Some are essential for a pilgrimage, others can be omitted without loss. A well-produced guide is essential.

What encourages so many men and women to give up precious holiday time to make an annual pilgrimage, returning year after year? Regulars come because it is a Holy Place, offering an annual moment to strengthen faith. It is not 'fun' in a secular sense, but it is fully alive. Life emerges from the thread of love, self-giving love, suffering love, bonding all pilgrims. Here we meet brothers and sisters from every part of the world, of all conditions and backgrounds, ages and languages.

Lourdes as an isolated frontier town was transformed by the visions of the Virgin Mary to Bernadette Soubirous between February and July 1858. Barely a teenager at the time, she was illiterate, already suffering the disease that would kill her, born into a family living in poverty. She did not know what to make of the visions but was so strong in her conviction that her story remained consistent in spite of intense questioning by clergy and others. The lady of the vision asked for a chapel, for pilgrims, for prayer and for penance. Healing miracles occurred and numbers grew quickly. At 21, Bernadette entered a convent at Nevers, where she died at the age of 35, suffering greatly to the end. Her life challenges our values.

She showed how we can find happiness by accepting our lot, however fragile and insignificant, by finding God in the present moment. Holiness comes from seeing God alive within and around us however poor, fragile and sinful we are. That is the healing offered at Lourdes.

The Lady who appeared to Bernadette, Mary of the Immaculate Conception, summarized this in two phrases associated with her in the New Testament: 'I am the handmaid of the Lord, let what you have said be done to me' and 'nothing is impossible to God' (Luke 1:37–8).

I commend this guide to all pilgrims. It will help to orientate you in Lourdes and ensure you make the most of your visit.

The Right Reverend Timothy Wright, O S B
Abbot of Ampleforth Abbey (1997–2005)

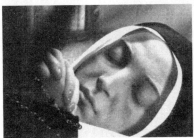

Bernadette Soubirous

St Bernadette's casket

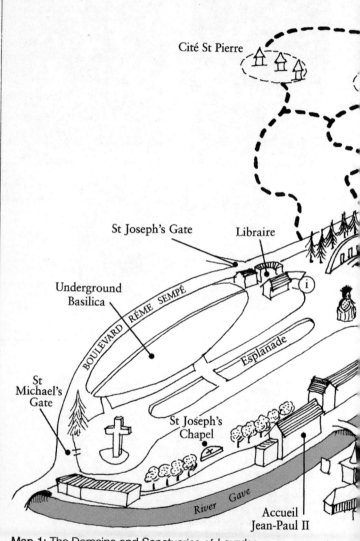

Cité St Pierre

St Joseph's Gate

Libraire

Underground
Basilica

BOULEVARD RÉME SEMPÉ

Esplanade

St
Michael's
Gate

St Joseph's
Chapel

River Gave

Accueil
Jean-Paul II

Map 1: The Domaine and Sanctuaries of Lourdes

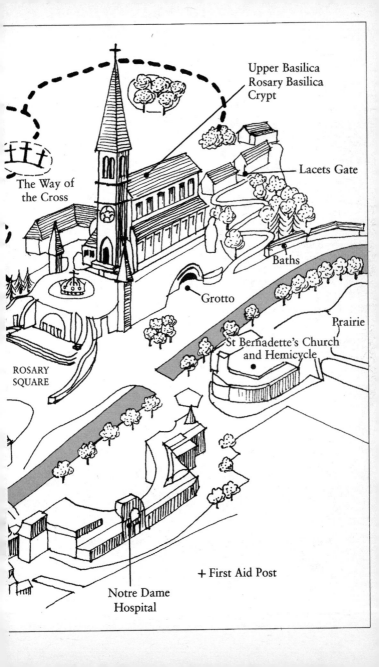

Upper Basilica
Rosary Basilica
Crypt

Lacets Gate

The Way of
the Cross

Baths

Grotto

Prairie

St Bernadette's Church
and Hemicycle

ROSARY
SQUARE

Notre Dame
Hospital

+ First Aid Post

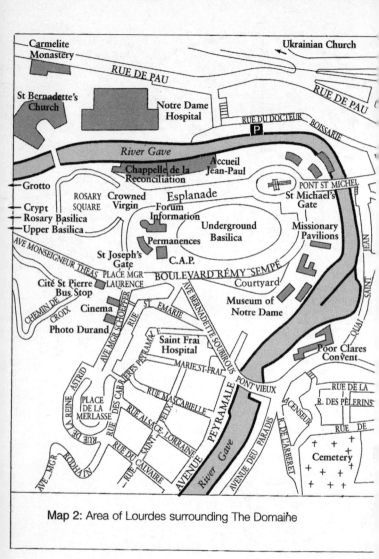

Map 2: Area of Lourdes surrounding The Domaine

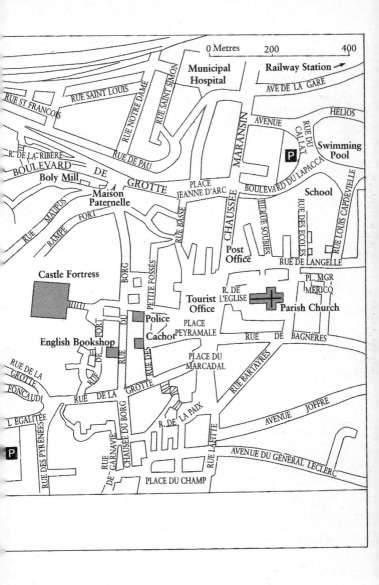

Map 3: Lourdes and surrounding area.

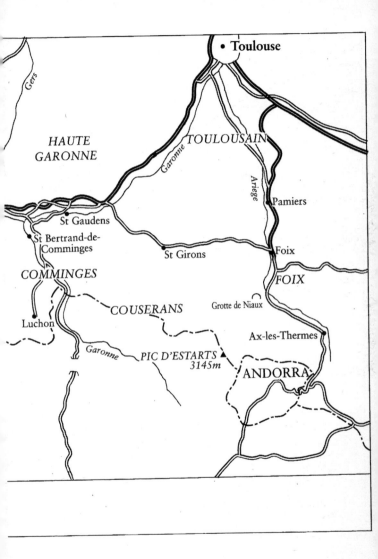

1

Introduction

Lourdes, even though not centuries old, is after Jerusalem and Rome, one of the great places of pilgrimage in the Christian world, and is particularly special in giving us the message of Lourdes, which quite simply is the Good News of the gospel. It is indicative of the importance of this shrine of pilgrimage that there are 24 replicas of the Grotto all over the world, underlining the belief in what took place in 1858 in this small, quiet town set in the foothills of the Pyrenees.

Lourdes is not a tourist attraction and as such one should not visit it as a spectator. It is vital to come as a pilgrim – either to join the day pilgrimage programme or to come for longer as part of a diocesan or parish pilgrimage. It is a place of prayer, of repentance, of renewal, of reflection, and above all a place where so many sick people find comfort.

Bernadette Soubirous was just 14 years old when the momentous events took place in 1858, which led Lourdes to become the shrine we see today. The experiences of this young girl during which she witnessed 18 apparitions between 11 February and 16 July have truly left the most remarkable legacy. 'The Lady', which was the way she so carefully described Our Lady, chose a young shepherd girl as the foundation of this extraordinary place full of Christian hope.

I first came to Lourdes as a newly engaged 20-year-old in 1965. It had an enormous impact on me especially as we were involved in looking after quite a number of sick pilgrims, seeing to their day-to-day essential needs. One stretcher case in particular comes to mind: Robert could do nothing for himself and it was my job each morning to give him his breakfast. As I broke off pieces of a somewhat dry croissant to put in his mouth he had something to tell me – I listened hard as he was very difficult to understand. His message was that coming to Lourdes made him feel fortunate as he saw so many other people much worse than himself.

Going to Lourdes has become an important part of our family life, and now nearly 40 years later we regularly go on pilgrimage, as do our four sons, and as a family we total some 76 pilgrimages between us. In those early days we assembled at London's Victoria Station with all our sick pilgrims and helpers; next stop was the ferry port of Folkestone, where we transferred everyone, including many wheelchair and stretcher-bound pilgrims, on to the ferry to Boulogne. Once in France, we boarded a large train equipped with couchettes for the sick, and a full restaurant-car service. There was just time to nip into the café at the station (which stayed open for us at 2 a.m.!) to have a quick coffee (and perhaps a cognac!) before setting off on our long journey down to Lourdes. As we approached the railway station at Lourdes, with the mountains in the background, everyone on the train joined in the singing of the Lourdes hymn – 'Ave Maria'.

This guidebook is intended to help the pilgrim, both before going to Lourdes and while there. You will find a comprehensive A–Z list of the essence of all the important places to visit, which gives both practical advice alongside essential information with some religious and historical background. There are maps to help you find your way around, along with local knowledge and other interesting venues to visit in the area. Also included are a few appropriate prayers and hymns, and most importantly a short history of the story of Bernadette.

I shall pass through this world but once. Any good that I can do, or any kindness that I can show to any human being, let me do it now, let me not defer nor neglect it, for I shall not pass this way again.

2

Practical Information for Visitors to Lourdes

HOW TO GET TO LOURDES

Lourdes is 700 miles from the Channel ports (Calais and Boulogne) and as such a long car journey, but with a stopover or two on the way it can be a pleasant drive through agreeable country-side, down the western side of France. Chartres, the chateaux of the Loire, Cognac, the Dordogne, the Gouffre de Padirac (with its amazing abyss leading into an underground river), provide a few suggestions to visit en route, not to mention the extensive wine-growing regions of the Loire and Bordeaux.

Lourdes is situated some 420 metres above sea level and is part of the Béout chain of the Pyrenees (see Map 3 at the front of the book). It is a town of 20,000 inhabitants, and is divided into two parts by the River Gave: the old town above the castle fortress on the east side; and the shrines of the Domaine and nearby hotels, cafés and souvenir shops over the Pont Vieux on the west side.

Coming with a pilgrimage to Lourdes presents no problem as it is customary for flights, train journeys or jumbulances to be arranged by your group when booking. The nearest airport is Tarbes-Lourdes-Pyrenees International Airport which is 10 kilometres from the centre of Lourdes, but from England and Ireland only charter flights land there. However, there are two daily return flights from Paris Orly Sud airport all year (tel: +33 [0] 1 48 34 93 90).

Pau-Pyrenees Airport is 40 kilometres from Lourdes and has flights all the year round, but it is limited by the destinations that fly there. Toulouse Airport has regular scheduled flights to and from London airports; there is a two-and-a-half-hour train journey on to Lourdes from Toulouse.

There are four daily return TGV trains from Paris between April and October and three from November to March, leaving from Gare Montparnasse, 17 Boulevard Vaugirard tel: +33 [0] 1 45 38 52 29). It is a five-and-a-half-hour journey via Bordeaux.

WHICH PILGRIMAGE?

There are a host of English-speaking pilgrimages that come to Lourdes each year, many of which are run by local dioceses, but there are also smaller groups who go under the umbrella of their local Catholic church. It is more likely for the diocesan pilgrimages to take sick people for care in the hospitals, and to find out dates of these visit the Internet site of the Sanctuary of Our Lady of Lourdes where you will find the Pilgrimage Calendar for Dioceses: http://www.lourdes-france.com

There is a Handicapped Children's Pilgrimage and a Military Pilgrimage, along with pilgrimages run by a number of schools and other organizations. There is no facility to find out information for all the pilgrimages that go to Lourdes, so the best advice is either to approach your local Catholic church or to get in touch with your local Catholic Diocesan Office, who should be able to give you the right point of contact. Do remember that all Christian denominations are welcome, and that there are a number of pilgrims from other faiths who come to Lourdes.

TOURIST INFORMATION AND SERVICES

Lourdes Tourist Information Office Place Peyramale, BP 17, 65101 Lourdes. Open all the year round, Monday to Saturday. Tel: +33 (0) 5 62 42 77 40. Fax: +33 (0) 5 62 94 60 95. E-mail: info@lourdes-infotourisme.com http://www.lourdes-infotourisme

Lourdes welcomes nationalities from all over the world but the six languages used in most places are French, English, German, Italian, Spanish and Dutch.

Accommodation There are a great number of hotels to choose from in Lourdes (see list on page 8 for a selection of four- and three-star hotels). Other hotels can be found at the back of the *Lourdes Magazine* or through the Lourdes Tourist Information Office.

Banks There are no banks in the new town, but cross the river at Pont Vieux and a short walk up Rue de la Grotte will bring you into the old town and the main shopping centre. Banks are open from 8.30 a.m. to 12 p.m. from 2 p.m. to 5 p.m., but most have a 24-hour cash-point facility.

Banque Nationale de
Paris, 2, Place de l'Eglise,
Rue St Pierre
Banque Populaire,
2, Rue de la Halle
Banque Courtois,
20, Place du Marcadal
Banque Inchauspe,
3, Place du Marcadal
Caisse d'Eoargne,
17, Place du Marcadal
Crédit Lyonnais,
11, Rue St Pierre
Crédit Mutuel,
19, Place du Marcadal
Société Générale,
53, Rue de la Grotte
Crédit Agricole, 11, Place
du Champ Commun

Shops   Shops and chemists
are normally open from
8 a.m. to 12 p.m. and from
2 p.m. to 6.30 p.m.
However, most souvenir
shops are open all day, and
some quite late into the
evening.

Bureaux de change
Open during the season
(1 April–31 October).
   28, Avenue Bernadette
   Soubirous
   63, Boulevard de la Grotte
   104, Rue de la Grotte
   (open on Sundays)

Car rental services
   Avis (at the railway
   station).
   Tel: +33 (0) 5 62 42 12 97.
   Fax: +33 (0) 5 62 94 57 09.
   CSA, 59, Avenue
   Alexandre Marqui.
   Tel: +33 (0) 5 62 94 24 18
   Location auto – Pyrenees,
   avenue du Monge.

Tel: +33 (0) 5 62 94 23 08.
Fax: +33 (0) 5 62 46 13 30.
Rent-A-Car, 25, Avenue
Alexandre Marqui.
Tel: +33 (0) 5 62 94 16 32.
Fax: +33 (0) 5 59 40 16 76.

Distances   1 mile = 0.62
kilometres; 5 miles =
8 kilometres; 62.14 miles =
100 kilometres.

Disabled access   Wheelchair
access is available in most
places, but it must be
remembered that there are
a lot of hills in Lourdes.
Comfortable footwear is
recommended at all times.

Electrical appliances   Plug
sockets are two-pronged, so
a travel adaptor is required.
These are available at most
airports and travel shops.

Finance   The Euro is the
currency used throughout
France.

Health   It is essential to
carry a current E111 form
in France; it must be dated
the year you are travelling to
be accepted by any hospital.
E111 forms are available
from your local Post Office.

Market   Rue Lafitte (Old
Town).   There is a covered
market in a splendid late
nineteenth-century building –
'Les Halles' – open every
morning. As well as excellent
meat, fruit and dairy
products, it is a good place
to buy local wares.

Post Office   Rue de
Langelle. Open Monday to

Friday from 8.30 a.m. to 6.30 p.m.; Saturday from 8.30 a.m. to 12 p.m.

NB There is also a small Post Office kiosk outside St Joseph's Gate plus postboxes. Open Monday to Friday from 10 a.m. to 12.15 p.m. and from 3 p.m. to 5.15 p.m. (closed on Saturdays).

Public conveniences There are public lavatories situated around Lourdes, particularly within and immediately outside the Domaine, and they are well signposted – most have disabled facilities.

Telephones The closest public telephones to the Domaine are immediately outside the entrance to St Joseph's Gate, near the Forum Information, and outside the entrance to St Michael's Gate. Most public call-boxes take both coins and phonecards, available from the Post Office, railway station, tobacconists and the Domaine bookshop. To telephone the United Kingdom, dial 0044 and then the number you require minus the first 0. Mobile telephone reception is good in Lourdes.

Useful telephone numbers and addresses

General Hospital, 3, Avenue Alexandre Marqui.
Tel: +33 (0) 5 62 42 42 42.
Duty doctors and chemists (Sundays and Bank Holidays).
Tel: +33 (0) 5 62 42 72 72.
Police station, 7, Rue du Baron Duprat.
Tel: +33 (0) 5 62 42 72 72.
Bus station.
Tel: +33(0) 5 62 94 31 15.
There is a bus that departs every 15 minutes from outside St Joseph's Gate, to the Old Town and railway station.
Taxis Place de la Gare (the railway station).
Tel: +33(0)5 62 94 31 30
Place Monseigneur Laurence.
Tel: +33 (0) 5 62 94 31 35
Airport Tarbes-Lourdes-Pyrenees International Airport, 6527 Juillan, Tarbes.
Tel: +33 (0) 5 62 32 92 22.
Fax: +33 (0) 5 62 32 93 71.
E-mail: aeroport@tarbes-lourdes.aeroport.fr
http://www.tarbes-lourdes.aeropost.fr
Pau-Pyrenees Airport, 64230 Uzein.
Tel: +33 (0) 5 59 33 33 00.
Fax: +33 (0) 5 59 33 33 05.
E-mail: contact@pau.aeroport.fr
http://www.pau.aeroport.fr
Lourdes railway station, 33, Avenue de la Gare.
Tel: +33 (0) 5 62 46 45 62.
Fax: +33 (0) 5 62 46 45 26.
http://www.sncf.com

Weather The weather can be unpredictable in Lourdes, to say the least. Summers are usually hot, but interspersed with violent thunderstorms accompanied by torrential rain. Being 2,000 feet up in the Pyrenees, the temperature all the year round is lower than the average in the rest of the South of France, and can be very changeable.

THE BASQUES

The origin of the Basques and their language, the oldest in Europe, is not definitively known. Of the seven Basque provinces three are in France and four in Spain, with an estimated population of about one and a half million. The Basques call themselves Euskaldunak, their country Euskadi and their language Euskara, and thus have succeeded in retaining their identity, their religious and family customs, their arts and their folklore. Euskara is unconnected to Latin and does not relate to any other known language group having survived unaffected by the arrival of more recent languages. However, the Basques are bilingual in French, which has now become their primary language. Since Napoleonic times when the government in Paris eliminated regional differences, this area of France called the Pays Basque has become a part of the Department of Hautes-Pyrenees.

Basque architecture is quite distinctive; the whitewashed, partly timbered houses, many with a first-floor balcony, help to form picturesque towns and villages in this scenically beautiful part of France. With a higher than average rainfall than the rest of the South of France, the Pays Basque is lushly green, and the gardens are full of the ever-popular hydrangea and other brightly coloured flowers. Village festivals are held frequently; a range of entertainment is provided, including colourful folk dances, poetry-reading, wood-cutting contests and the local sport, *pelota*. This vigorous team game has a number of variations: sometimes it is played with a small racquet; at others with a scoop attached to a glove. It can be played on a pitch next to a high wall called a *fronton*, scoring points by the ball being struck against the wall; it can also be played indoors – this is known as *en trinquet*. The team can consist of two, three or five players; the five-team version called *rebot* is probably the origin of 'Fives', started in England in the nineteenth century.

Look out for Basque linen in the form of tablecloths and napkins, available in a range of colours. These make useful and attractive presents to take home.

LOCAL FOOD AND DRINK SPECIALITIES

Cured ham from Bayonne and tuna from St-Jean-de-Luz are famous. The area is renowned for its river fish, especially trout. Tome de Brebis is the local cheese and the local goats cheese is also to be recommended. Two wines to look out for are Irouleguy from the Basque country and Jurançon from the Pau area; the local liqueur is *Izarra* (meaning 'star'), which is an armagnac-based liqueur with herbs and honey. It comes in green and yellow varieties, the yellow being slightly milder. Watch out for 'liqueurs des Pyrenees' in attractive stone bottles; these are fruit based, with blackberry, raspberry, blueberry, juniper, cassis and wild strawberry to select from. High mountain honey is a speciality, and is delicious.

HOTELS

There are many hotels in Lourdes, in fact the highest number of any town in France other than Paris. A few four-star hotels are complemented by a larger number of three-star ones, which mainly offer full board; a selection of these, all of which are within walking distance of the Domaine are listed below. Most offer some disabled rooms, and also off-street garage parking. There are also two-star and one-star hotels, and Bed and Breakfast accommodation. For a full list of hotels apply to the Lourdes Tourist Information Office (see page 4). Some hotels are open all the year round, but a number only during the pilgrimage season – 1 April to 31 October.

NB The star rating of these hotels does not reflect the equivalent standard of service you would normally expect, but nonetheless they provide adequate and comfortable accommodation and have either a shower or bathroom en suite.

Four Star

Hotel Eliséo, 4–6, Rue de la Reine Astrid. 204 air-conditioned rooms.
Tel: +33 (0) 5 62 41 41 41.
Fax: 33 (0) 5 62 41 41 50.
E-mail: *eliseo@cometo lourdes.com*
Open from 1 February to 15 December.

Grande Hotel de la Grotte, 66 to 68, Rue de la Grotte. 82 rooms.
Tel: +33 (0) 5 62 94 58 87.
Fax: +33 (0) 5 62 94 20 50.
E-mail: *info@hoteldelagrotte.com*
Under the same management for four generations.

Grande Hotel Moderne, 21, Avenue Bernadette Soubirous. 110 rooms.
Tel: +33 (0) 5 62 94 12 32.
Fax: +33 (0) 6 62 42 07 17.

E-mail: *contact@ hotelmodernelourdes.com*

Hotel Vesuvio, 75, Rue de la Grotte. 25 rooms.
Tel: +33 (0) 5 62 46 32 10.
Fax: +33 (0) 5 62 46 32 20.
E-mail: *Hotel.vesuvio@ wanadoo.fr*

Three Star

Hotel des Ambassadeurs, 2, Rue du Docteur Boissarie. 48 rooms.
Tel: +33 (0) 5 62 94 32 85.
Fax: +33 (0) 5 62 94 46 90.
E-mail: *ramboisier@wanadoo.fr*

Grand Hotel d' Angleterre, 4, Rue St Joseph. 56 rooms.
Tel: +33 (0) 5 62 94 00 15.
Fax: +33 (0) 5 62 94 66 45.
E-mail: *hotel.angleterre@ wanadoo.fr*

Hotel Arcades, 13, Avenue du Paradis. 216 rooms.
Tel: +33 (0) 5 62 94 20 59.
Fax: +33 (0) 5 62 94 72 17.
E-mail: *arcadeslourdes@ wanadoo.fr*

Hotel Ariane, 4 Rue Saint Félix. 144 rooms.
Tel: +33 (0) 5 62 94 22 70.
Fax: +33 (0) 5 62 42 03 38.
E-mail: *ariane@sudfr.com*

Hotel Astoria-Vatican, 93–95, Rue de la Grotte. 151 rooms.
Tel: 33 (0) 5 62 94 06 96.
Fax: +33 (0) 5 62 94 40 41.
E-mail: *info@astoria.fr*

Best Western Christina, 42, Avenue Peyramale. 200 rooms.
Tel: +33 (0) 5 62 94 26 11.
Fax: +33 (0) 5 62 94 97 09.

Hotel de Bourgogne et Bretagne, 20, Avenue Peyramale. 85 rooms.
Tel: +33 (0) 5 62 94 49 50.
Fax: +33 (0) 5 62 94 39 28.
E-mail: *hotel-bourgogne-bre- tagne@wanadoo.fr*

Hotel Christ Roi, 9, Rue Monseigneur Rodhain.
180 rooms.
Tel: +33 (0) 5 62 94 24 98.
Fax: +33 (0) 5 62 94 17 65.

Hotel Corona, 4, Rue du Calvaire. 65 rooms.
Tel: +33 (0) 5 62 94 23 30.
Fax: +33 (0) 5 62 94 83 34.
E-mail: *contact@ hotel-corona-lourdes.com*

Hotel Esplanade Eden, 12, Esplanade du Paradis.
140 rooms.
Tel: +33 (0) 5 62 94 42 23.
Fax: +33 (0) 5 62 94 81 61.
E-mail: *hotel-esplanade@ wanadoo.fr*

Hotel Excelsior, 83, Boulevard de la Grotte.
Tel: +33 (0) 5 62 94 02 05.
Fax: +33 (0) 5 62 94 82 88.
E-mail: *hotel.excelsior@ wanadoo.fr*

Hotel Florida, 3, Rue des Carrières Peyramale. 117 rooms.
Tel: +33 (0) 5 62 94 51 15.
Fax: +33 (0) 5 62 94 69 49.
E-mail: *flo_aca_mira_hotels@ hotmail.com*

Hotel du Gave, 28, Avenue Peyramale. 60 rooms.
Tel: +33 (0) 5 62 94 90 11.
Fax: +33 (0) 5 62 94 94 94.

Comfort Hotel Gloria, 3, Rue du Calvaire. 91 rooms.
Tel: +33 (0) 5 62 94 23 48.
Fax: +33 (0) 5 62 94 85 55.
E-mail: *hotel-gloria@wanadoo.fr*

Hotel d'Irlande, 21 Rue Ste Marie. 72 rooms.
Tel: +33 (0) 5 62 94 04 32.
Fax: +33 (0) 5 62 94 43 59.
E-mail: *hotel.irlande@wanadoo.fr*

Hotel Lécuyer La Source, 8, Rue du Docteur Boissarie. 201 rooms.
Tel: +33 (0) 5 62 94 26 24.
Fax: +33 (0) 5 62 94 55 17.
E-mail: *hotel.lecuyer.lourdes@ gofornet.com*

Hotel Lys de Marie, 18, Avenue Peyramale. 101 rooms.
Tel: +33 (0) 5 62 94 20 53.
Fax: +33 (0) 5 62 94 66 90.
E-mail: *info@lyshotel.fr*

Hotel Madonna, 16, Avenue Peyramale. 74 rooms.
Tel: +33 (0) 5 62 94 21 43.
Fax: +33 (0) 5 62 94 88 89.

Hotel Myosotis, 5, Rue de la Reine Astrid. 50 rooms.
Tel: +33 (0) 5 62 94 04 02.
Fax: +33 (0) 5 62 94 84 32.
E-mail: *direction@ hotelmyosotis.com*

Hotel National, 1, Rue Saint Félix. 111 rooms.
Tel: +33 (0) 5 62 94 02 17.
Fax: +33 (0) 5 62 94 85 18.

E-mail: *info@lyshotel.fr*

Hotel Notre-Dame de Lourdes, 30, Avenue Bernadette Soubirous. 75 rooms.
Tel: +33 (0) 5 62 94 22 97.
Fax: +33 (0) 5 62 94 62 99.

Hotel de Paris, 5 and 7, Rue Ste Marie. 92 rooms.
Tel: +33 (0) 5 62 94 21 04.
Fax: +33 (0) 5 62 94 94 58.
E-mail: *hotel-de-paris@ wanadoo.fr*

Hotel des Pays-Bas, 11, Rue Louis Pomès. 62 rooms.
Tel: +33 (0) 5 62 94 16 66.
Fax: +33 (0) 5 62 94 20 84.
E-mail: *Hotel.paysbas.Lourdes@ wanadoo.fr*

Hotel Sainte-Suzanne, 24, Avenue Peyramale. 85 rooms.
Tel: +33 (0) 5 62 94 67 40.
Fax: +33 (0) 5 62 94 60 66.
E-mail: *hotel-st-suzanne@ sudfr.com*

Hotel Saint-Georges, 34, Avenue Peyramale. 52 rooms.
Tel: +33 (0) 5 62 94 78 32.
Fax: +33 (0) 5 62 94 81 62.
E-mail: *hotel@hotelalourdes.com*

3

The Story of Bernadette

LOURDES BEFORE 1858

In the first half of the nineteenth century and at the time of the Apparations, Lourdes was a small garrison town of some 4,500 inhabitants situated in the foothills of the Pyrenees on the River Gave. Since the eleventh century the town had been recognized mainly for its castle, which became the principal residence of the Counts of Bigorre, their lands having been elevated to the status of County in the ninth century. From here they could defend their frontier, and thereby protect the trading between the mountain dwellers and the inhabitants of the plain. In the thirteenth and fourteenth centuries Lourdes had been occupied by English forces on two different occasions for a period of over 50 years each, and by the seventeenth century the castle had become the property of the Crown under Henry IV of Navarre. It was also used as a state prison during the French Revolution.

It was an unremarkable town although up to date and progressive for its size with the bulk of the population consisting of agricultural workers and slate quarry workers. Lourdes was, nonetheless, a busy place, being the seat of the local magistrates court and housing a number of government offices. There was a corps of influential people who included members of the professional classes, civil servants and the landed gentry, along with shopkeepers and local craftsmen. They boasted printing their own local newspaper, and had formed a progressive free-thinkers club who met at Café Français in the Place du Marcadal twice a day.

On the eastern side where the fast-flowing River Lapaca ran were five mills, each competing for business from the wheat harvest. And so, with its own parish church and convent, and the population in the main practising Catholics, it was in this small uneventful town situated in beautiful natural surroundings, that the following events took place.

11

THE SOUBIROUS FAMILY

François Soubirous was born in 1807; having gone to help Claire Castérot, a young widow, run Boly Mill, in 1843 he married her younger daughter Louise and they had five children. The eldest of these was Bernadette, born on 7 January 1844. François was a miller by trade, but being no businessman and allowing customers too much credit, he was unable to make a success of the mill. When he could no longer pay the rent he and the family had no alternative but to leave in 1854. The following year a cholera epidemic hit Lourdes claiming 38 lives. Bernadette was also afflicted, but made a full recovery, although the illness left her with asthma from which she suffered for the rest of her life. Soon afterwards Claire Castérot died leaving François and Louise 900 francs, and so for a short time they rented the mill at Arcizac-ez-Angles. More bad luck was on the way when the harvest of 1856 failed following a severe drought, and once again the family were on the move to Rives House, a mere hovel. Not even being able to pay this minimal rent and thus penniless and homeless they moved to the Cachot, the punishment cell of an old prison, a place of misery and squalor, and quite inadequate for bringing up a family. (This has now been turned into a museum, and is a must for every pilgrim who comes to Lourdes [see page 38].)

In 1857 once again hardship hit François Soubirous when he was accused of stealing a bag of flour, but after a week in prison he was released through lack of evidence. He was now at an all-time low having been reduced from miller to pauper and suspected thief with no social status for himself or his family.

It was at this time that Bernadette spent a few months in Bartrès, four miles away, staying with the Laguës family near to her aunt. She helped mind the sheep and did household chores, but living on the farm away from her family made her homesick and, in January 1858, she returned to her family in Lourdes. She was thus able to attend the class held by the Sisters of Charity of Nevers for poor children as she had found great difficulty in learning to read and write, and she desperately wanted to receive her First Communion being by now much older than the other children who had received theirs. She had already shown from an early age that she had immense faith in God, and when she was told she was stupid because she was unable to learn her Catechism, she whispered that at least she 'would always know how to love the good God'.

On Thursday 11 February 1858 when she was just 14 years old, together with her sister Toinette and friend Jeanne Abadie, Bernadette left the Cachot to collect firewood at the foot of a hill called Massabielle, meaning old rock, where there was a small cave or grotto where cattle and pigs sheltered. Toinette and Jeanne kicked off their wooden shoes and waded across the brook in search of dead wood, leaving Bernadette hesitating because of the cold. Just as she was removing her stockings, she heard what sounded like a strong wind and, as she looked towards the grotto, she noticed that the vegetation growing beneath the higher opening was tossing, though nothing else moved.

To her amazement she saw a figure in the opening – a lady of small stature and incomparable beauty. The lady was surrounded by light and inclined her head graciously as if inviting Bernadette to approach. She put out her hands, too, a little distance from her body, and on her right arm could be seen a rosary with large white beads on what seemed a golden chain. Bernadette felt frightened, and yet she did not want to run away. She was fascinated,

experiencing a mysterious attraction and quite naturally she took out her own rosary and started to recite the prayers. The vision lasted about a quarter of an hour and, as Bernadette finished the prayers, quite suddenly the lady disappeared.

On the way home, Bernadette told Toinette what she had seen, and although her sister promised secrecy, she did not keep her secret and that evening the Soubirous family entered into what was to become an extremely vexing and puzzling period of their lives with much anguish to follow.

The vision was to be the first of 18 apparitions over the next five months (see page 14), frequently with many people in attendance out of curiosity, as by now the story of 'the lady' was the talking point of everyone in Lourdes. The visions were varied in their content: some gave Bernadette definite direction, while others were silent. It was during the thirteenth apparition that Bernadette was instructed to ask the priests to build a chapel by the grotto for people to process there, and this is the heart of Lourdes today. Possibly the most significant one was the sixteenth appearance when the Lady disclosed herself as the Immaculate Conception.

Following the outcome of the inquiry with Monseigneur Laurence declaring the Apparitions as genuine, the Soubirous parents moved to the Lacadé Mill where they lived until they died – Louise on 8 December 1866 and François on 4 March 1871. Although it has been called the family home, Bernadette visited but never actually lived there; by now she was with the Sisters of Charity's hospice school, from where soon after she was to enter the convent in Nevers in July 1866.

THE APPARITIONS

The First Apparition

The first apparition took place on 11 February 1858. At About 11 a.m. Bernadette, along with her sister Toinette and friend Jeanne Abadies left the Cachot in search of firewood. The other two went on ahead crossing a brook near the River Gave to reach the foot of the Massabielle hill (meaning, old rock) where there was a small cave or grotto. Bernadette lingered because of the cold, and as she was removing her stockings she heard a sound like a strong wind; looking towards the grotto she saw the vegetation tossing in an opening above it. To her astonishment she saw a figure, a lady dressed in white with a white veil and blue sash around her waist holding a rosary of white beads on a golden chain. The Lady moved the rosary beads between her fingers, but made no sound. She signalled for Bernadette to approach, but she didn't dare to do so, and quite suddenly the lady disappeared.

The Second Apparition

On 14 February Bernadette returned to the grotto for the second time. Having persuaded her mother to let her go, she took some holy water with her from the parish church to throw towards the apparition. There were about ten people present including her sister and friend. When the Lady appeared Bernadette threw the holy water towards her searching for some response. The Lady simply smiled back at her, and remained silent.

The Third Apparition

Four days later on 18 February, the day after Ash Wednesday, the third apparition took place. This was one of the four longest appearances of the Lady and for the first time she spoke. There were several important people present as Bernadette asked the Lady to write down what she wanted of her. In response, the Lady declined but spoke instead, and asked Bernadette to come to the grotto every day for the next 15 days. 'I do not promise you happiness in this world, but in the next,' she told Bernadette.

The Fourth Apparition

The following day, on Friday 19 February, Bernadette visited the grotto with her mother, Louise, and her Aunt Bernarde. This was the first time that Bernadette had brought a blessed candle with her, which she continued to do up until the sixteenth apparition when the Lady declared herself as the Immaculate Conception. There was a small gathering on this occasion when the Lady appeared in silence with no message, and as ever only Bernadette saw her.

The Fifth Apparition

On 20 February Bernadette returned to the grotto with her mother at about 6 a.m. with 30 or so people present. There was little to note in this apparition as the Lady did not speak, although Bernadette was full of ecstasy.

The Sixth Apparition

Crowds were now beginning to follow Bernadette to the grotto, and on Sunday 21 February the Lady appeared to her giving her the message to pray for sinners. It appeared that Bernadette cried during this apparition.

The Seventh Apparition

Early in the morning of 23 February, Bernadette returned to the grotto having been disappointed that the Lady had not appeared on the previous day. Some 250 people were present hoping to witness for themselves what Bernadette saw, as the seventh apparition took place in silent prayer. Later she was to disclose that the Lady imparted three personal secrets on this occasion with instructions that she must reveal them to no one.

The Eighth Apparition

On 24 February, the Lady appeared and told Bernadette to crawl on her knees into the grotto and kiss the ground as a sign of repentance for sinners. This message was repeated several times in the future, and this was when the penitential phase of the Apparitions began: 'Repentance, repentance, repentance'.

The Ninth Apparition

At about 5 a.m. on 25 February Bernadette visited the grotto accompanied by her aunts with around 300 people present. The Lady continued her theme of penance from the previous day, but this time told Bernadette to go to the spring to take a drink and wash herself, and to eat some grass near the spring. As there was no spring to be seen, she went towards the river, but the finger directed her back to beneath the rock. Bernadette put her hand where there was a little dirty water, and after scratching at the surface several times was able to find clean water to drink.

The Tenth Apparition

With no apparition on Friday 26 February, 800 people gathered near the grotto when the tenth apparition took place on 27 February. Bernadette saw the Lady, drank from the spring and, as before, repeated the same gestures of repentance and said the Rosary.

The Eleventh Apparition

On Sunday 28 February, at 7 a.m., the Lady repeated her earlier message about the need for prayer and penance. Nearly 1,100 people were present, including Commandant Renault who had been sent to report on these extraordinary events by Baron Massy, the Prefect of Tarbes.

The Twelfth Apparition

The story of these happenings at the grotto in Lourdes was now spreading, and each day the crowds increased. On 1 March a priest, Abbé Antoine Dézirat,

and the Mayor of Ossen, Jean Vergez, were present when Bernadette saw the Lady for the twelfth time, although on this occasion she did not speak.

The Thirteenth Apparition

'Go and tell the Priests to build a chapel here and let the people come to this place in procession.' This command from the Lady on 2 March led to Bernadette coming under severe scrutiny from Father Peyramale, the parish priest of Lourdes, and when Bernadette visited him with this request he demanded to know the Lady's name.

The Fourteenth Apparition

After the disappointment of no appearance of the Lady on the morning of Wednesday 3 March, Bernadette returned later that evening having spent the day at school. This time all was well, and the Lady repeated her command to build a chapel, but again Father Peyramale asked for some sort of miraculous sign as proof of the apparition.

The Fifteenth Apparition

At 4 a.m. on Thursday 4 March four policemen were ordered to take watch at the grotto. This was the last of the 15 days that the Lady had requested Bernadette to visit and on this occasion

1. A view over the Underground Basilica towards Rosary Square

2. The Rosary Basilica and Rosary Square

3. The Crown on the dome of Rosary Basilica to commemorate the Crowning of Our Lady of Lourdes

4. The Bas-relief of Our Lady of the Rosary and St Dominic

5. Candle votive stands

6. St Bernadette's Church

7. The Grotto

8. Boly Mill where Bernadette was born

9. The Cachot where the Soubirous family lived at the time of the Apparitions

10. The Carmelite Chapel

11. The Ukrainian Church

12. The Castle Fortress

13. The twelfth Station of the Cross

14. The Parish Church in Lourdes Old Town

when Bernadette asked her name, the Lady simply smiled. The apparition lasted 45 minutes with the usual prayers and penitential gestures, and the crowd of over 7,000 people felt disappointment at the lack of something tangible occurring, although the local authorities were relieved that nothing untoward had taken place.

Between 5 and 24 March 1858 there was a break in the Apparitions when Bernadette ceased going to the grotto; she no longer felt the irresistible force inviting her. This time was spent preparing for her First Holy Communion at school while regaining her equilibrium after the events of the previous six weeks. The unexplained happenings were beginning to fade in people's memories, and Bernadette was returning to her former anonymity, until the Feast of the Annunciation when Bernadette felt a strong desire to return to the grotto. Following the sixteenth apparition there were intervals of ten days and three months between the final two visions.

The Sixteenth Apparition

On Thursday 25 March, three weeks after the last apparition, Bernadette returned to the grotto, and three times she asked the Lady who she was. On the fourth occasion the Lady replied in the Basque tongue, 'I am the Immaculate Conception.' This was the last time that the Lady spoke to Bernadette, and it was after this apparition, when Bernadette rushed to the priest's house to tell him the news, that Father Peyramale began to realize that the events at the grotto had some serious meaning.

It is of interest to note that it was not until 8 December 1853, only five years before these events, that the Pope had proclaimed to the world the doctrine that the Most Blessed Virgin Mary from the first instant of her conception – that is, of her presence in her mother's womb – had been preserved from all stain of original sin by a singular privilege and grace granted by God on account of the merits of Jesus Christ. It is therefore unlikely that Bernadette would have either understood or heard of this dogma; even great scholars of the time were puzzled by this concept.

The Seventeenth Apparition

Thirteen days later, on Wednesday 7 April, Bernadette visited the grotto and during this silent apparition she became so enraptured with her thoughts and prayers that she failed to notice that the flame of her candle was burning her fingers. Remarkably there was no trace of burns, and having examined her closely afterwards, Dr Dozous (a local physician and lifelong atheist) became convinced that something mysterious and supernatural had occurred, and converted to Christianity.

The Eighteenth Apparition

The grotto by now had been barricaded off (access to the Massabielle bank was barred) and a decree was published on 10 June prohibiting the taking of water from the spring at the grotto; it added that anyone contravening this law would be prosecuted. The local Police and Municipal Authorities were charged with enforcing this ordinance. It was therefore from the meadow on the other side of the River Gave that Bernadette saw the Lady for the last time on Friday 16 July, commenting that she looked more radiant than ever before.

It is important to know that Bernadette underwent frequent interrogations during the earlier apparitions and was even threatened with prison if she would not promise to stay away from the grotto. She remained calm and resolute throughout.

THE DEVELOPMENT OF LOURDES

Soon after the last apparition on 16 July 1858, an inquiry into these recent events was commissioned by the then Bishop of Tarbes, Monseigneur Bertrand Laurence. Throughout the events that had taken place at the grotto, Bernadette had frequently been questioned by the civil authorities, and this was now to be extended over the next four years to the Church elders. In the meantime, on 5 October 1858, Napoleon III, Emperor of France, had the grotto re-opened, and the following August actually came to visit. Unexplainable healings were already taking place, and every day significant crowds were gathering by the grotto. Lourdes was becoming a town of fame, soon to be a place of pilgrimage.

Life for Bernadette had become difficult, and in order to protect her from the constant attention of curious sightseers Father Peyramale asked the Sisters of Charity of Nevers to let her stay in the boarding house at their hospice school (the present General Hospital of Lourdes). This proved to be an excellent move, as Bernadette was now able to get to grips with her reading and writing which she had formerly been so slow to learn; in due course she was even able to write her own account of the Apparitions.

It was on 18 January 1862 that Monseigneur Laurence finally issued his verdict. 'We consider that the Immaculate Mary, Mother of God, really did appear to Bernadette Soubirous on 11 February 1858 and the following days, a total of 18 times, in the grotto at Massabielle near the town of Lourdes, that the Apparition possesses all the characteristics of truth, and that the faithful are justified in believing it to be genuine. We authorize within our diocese the worship of Our Lady of the Grotto of Lourdes.' His statement went on to authenticate the first seven miraculous cures.

Later that year on 14 October 1862, a team of labourers including Bernadette's father, François Soubirous, began building the Crypt, and it was from that point on that the whole concept of Lourdes as we see it today developed.

THE CONVENT AT NEVERS

On 7 July 1866, Bernadette arrived at Saint Gildard's Convent, the Mother House of the Sisters of Charity, in Nevers, 130 miles south of Paris, and on 29 July she took up her habit as Sister Marie-Bernard. She had a tough time during her novitiate because the Mistress of the Novices, not quite knowing how to treat her, decided to be twice as hard on Bernadette as on the other new sisters. Her situation was not helped by falling ill, and by 25 October she was allowed to take her vows in advance as she was thought to be on the verge of death. By February of the following year she had pulled through and on 30 October 1867 renewed her vows in the presence of the whole community.

Bernadette was to remain at the mother house where she assisted Sister Marthe Forest, the convent's nurse, until she herself became seriously ill and Bernadette took on the duties of chief nurse. Ill-health began to plague Bernadette and in 1873 she was relieved of her duties; from 1875 she became virtually bedridden.

When Father Peyramale died on 8 September 1877 Bernadette predicted her own death and it was two years later that she died at the age of 35, having now been given the last rites on four different occasions. She was buried in the grounds of the Convent where she remained until 30 years later when in 1909, due to part of the graveyard being resited, her remains were moved. The Sisters found they were able to lift Bernadette's body into a fresh coffin and deposit it unharmed in the new sarcophagus. Forty-six years after her death, on 18 April 1925, Bernadette's body was exhumed for the second time and examined by the commission appointed by the court of canonization. Her body was like that of one just dead and showed no normal process of decay; her internal organs remained in perfect condition. She was canonized on the Feast of the Immaculate Conception, 8 December 1933, by Pope Pius XI. Her body now lies in a glass reliquary in the main chapel of the Convent of Saint Gildard.

Information

This quiet, unassuming convent is well worth a visit should you be in the vicinity of Nevers on the River Loire just off the N7, 130 miles south of Paris. There is a small replica of the Grotto in the garden, and a delightfully laid-out museum of Bernadette's personal effects.

4

The Miracles

Jesus was teaching where there were Pharisees and teachers of the law sitting by, who had come from every village of Galilee and Judea and from Jerusalem; and the power of the Lord was with him to heal. And behold, men were bringing on a bed a man who was paralyzed, and they sought to bring him in and lay him before Jesus; but finding no way to bring him in, because of the crowd, they went up on the roof and let him down with his bed through the tiles into the midst before Jesus. And when he saw their faith he said, 'Man your sins are forgiven you.' And the scribes and the Pharisees began to question, saying, 'Who is this that speaks blasphemies?' When Jesus perceived their questionings, he answered them, 'Why do you question in your hearts? Which is easier, to say, "Your sins are forgiven you," or to say, "Rise and walk"? But that you may know that the Son of man has authority on earth to forgive sins' – he said to the man who was paralyzed – 'I say to you, rise, take up your bed and go home.' And immediately he rose before them, and took up that on which he lay, and went home, glorifying God. And amazement seized them all, and they glorified God and were filled with awe, saying, 'We have seen strange things today.'

Luke 5 : 17–26

We are all familiar with the miracles of the New Testament, such as Jesus' healing of the paralysed man demonstrating the power of God. The first miracles in Lourdes came about during and soon after the Apparitions took place, although Our Lady had told Bernadette to come in procession, to build a chapel, to pray for sinners, to do penance and to bathe and drink at the Grotto, with no intimation of cures.

Initially, the great pilgrimages to Lourdes from Paris did not bring sick pilgrims with them, but over a period of five years from 1875 the numbers grew from 50 to 500 due to the knowledge that local people in Lourdes were being cured, and by 1887 there were thousands of sick being brought to Lourdes each year. This growth was supported by the expansion of the Hospitaliers – the lay organization that looks after the sick in Lourdes – and the many volunteers who come to help.

To date there have been 66 authenticated cures out of some 6,800 recorded cases in Lourdes, among which many other inexplicable events have taken place. These cures are scrutinized extremely closely before being accepted, and go before an International Medical Bureau consisting of numerous doctors and medical scientists from throughout the world, both Christian and non-Christian. It takes several years to investigate these cases to ensure that the cure is permanent and not an illness in remission. Each case must prove beyond doubt that no medical explanation can be given for the cure which must be sudden, unforeseen and total, without any convalescence. The sickness prior to the cure must have been life-threatening, organic and objectively diagnosed.

It is notable that many of the early cures were for tuberculosis, as this was a widespread disease and prevalent in the late nineteenth and early twentieth centuries. Interestingly, no genetic cure has ever been recorded, but most infections and a number of rare diseases have been cured. Not all the cures have actually taken place in Lourdes itself. It is also a fact that 80% of miraculous cures have been to women. The Museum of the Miracles, which contains photographs and written explanations (in French), can be found on the first floor of the Accueil Jean-Paul II, situated alongside the Esplanade in the Domaine.

The first recorded miracle took place on 1 March 1858, and the most recent occurred on 9 October 1987, nearly 130 years later.

1 **Catherine Latapie** was born in 1820 and lived near Lourdes. She had suffered paralysis in her right hand following an accident, which made life as a young mother extremely difficult. On 1 March 1858 at the age of 38 she came to pray at the Grotto with her young children and bathed her arm in the water from the spring. She immediately regained full use of her fingers, but it was four years later before her cure was recognized. Her third child was born on the evening of her cure, and he later became a priest.

2 **Louis Bouriette**, born in 1804, seriously damaged his right eye following an explosion in the quarry where he worked in Lourdes in 1839; his brother was actually killed. In 1858, at the age of 54, having finally lost all sight in his right eye two years earlier, he visited the Grotto to wash his eye in the spring that Bernadette had made flow. He repeatedly bathed his eye while praying to Our Lady, and full vision was restored.

3 **Blaisette Cazenave** was born in 1808 and lived in Lourdes. At the age of 50, after many years of suffering from untreatable eye problems, she imitated the actions of Bernadette at the Grotto and drank from the spring and washed her face. After only the second time of drinking at the spring and washing her face, her eyelids healed and the sores disappeared, leaving her free of any pain and inflammation.

4 **Henri Busquet** was only 16 and could no longer bear the suffering from tuberculosis, which had been wrongly diagnosed as typhoid. The incorrect treatment he was given caused an abscess on his throat which developed into lesions, and in 1858 symptoms of an ulcer appeared at the base of his neck. While the family prayed around him, Henri was given a bandage soaked in Lourdes water, and the following day the ulcer and all other infections had completely gone.

5 **Justin Bouhort** was frequently ill since his birth in July 1856. Only two years of age, he was considered infirm and showed signs of growth deficiency; he had never walked. In July 1858 his mother took him to the Grotto to pray, even though by now the authorities had blocked off access. She said a prayer in front of the rock and with her child in her arms decided to bathe him in the pool. The considerable crowd screamed at her, accusing her of trying to kill the little boy, but when she got home, despite him being very weak, the child slept peacefully and in the days following he learnt to walk. His health improved and he survived into adulthood. On 8 December 1933 he attended Bernadette's canonization in Rome, and died two years later at the age of 79.

6 **Madeleine Rizan** was born in 1800 and had been bedridden for over 20 years due to being paralysed down her left side. All hopes of a cure had long since gone, and treatment had been withdrawn; she had even received Extreme Unction. When she was 58 and by

now praying for an easy death, her daughter brought her some Lourdes water. She drank a little and washed her face and body with it. Her paralysis immediately vanished, and she lived for another 11 years with no relapses.

7   **Marie Moreau** was 17 years old and living at Tartas in Les Landes. The previous year she contracted an illness that badly inflamed her eyes, and she was gradually losing her sight. Her father had read about the successful cure of Madeleine Rizan, and in November 1858 he went to Lourdes to get some water from the spring at the Grotto. On his return home, he poured the water on to a cloth which she put over her eyes, and the next day on removing the cloth she could see as perfectly as she could before her illness. Now able to re-continue with her studies, she later went on to marry.

8   **Pierre de Rudder**, born in 1822, had a leg crushed by a falling tree in 1867. The wound became badly infected, and amputation was recommended as any hopes of healing had been given up despite endless treatments. Eight years after his accident he made a pilgrimage to Oostacker (near Ghent, Belgium) where there is a replica of the Lourdes Grotto. Having left home an invalid, he returned on the same day without crutches as his bones had healed in just a few minutes; now 52 years old he was able to return to normal life.

9   **Joachime Dehant** was 29 when gangrene developed in her right leg, resulting from lesions that she had suffered from for at least ten years. She came to Lourdes in 1878 and took two baths in the water. After the second bath, all traces of her sores had disappeared and her skin was pink again. Following a third bath her foot regained a normal appearance, but it was another 30 years before her cure was proclaimed miraculous.

10   **Elisa Seisson** had suffered from chronic bronchitis and heart disease since the age of 21. Having been told that her condition was incurable she came to Lourdes in August 1882. On the first day she went to the Baths and when she came out the swellings on her leg had gone. After a peaceful night's sleep, she felt completely cured and she remained in good health for many years to come.

11   **Sister Eugénia** was born in 1855 and following the removal of her appendix suffered an abscess which led to peritonitis. Surgery was

ruled out and her state of health worsened as any treatment was ineffective. She managed to get to Lourdes in 1883 and went straight to the Grotto where she immediately felt a soothing of her symptoms. Later that afternoon, she felt cured, and went to the Baths, where all signs of illness disappeared. She was able to return to her convent and live to the rules of her Community once again.

12   **Sister Julienne** was only 25 and suffering from incurable tuberculosis. Her story nearly became forgotten as 35 years after she was cured in the Baths in Lourdes, an inquiry was set up; the Medical Bureau could find no explanation for this young nun's cure and the Bishop of Tulle, Monseigneur Nègre, deemed the cure as miraculous.

13   **Sister Joséphine Marie** came from a family of tuberculosis sufferers, and had lost two sisters and a brother from the disease. In July 1890 when she was 36 years old she came on a pilgrimage to Lourdes despite going against her doctor's advice. After her third immersion in the Baths she felt much better, and started to tell everyone she was cured. When she returned to the Community, that same doctor could not find any symptoms left from

her illness, and she went on to live an active life in the convent.

14   **Amélie Chagnon** was 13 years old when the pain in her knee was thought to be caused by growing pains. Later diagnosed with tuberculosis, which spread to her foot, she informed her doctor of her intended visit to Lourdes. Fortunately he agreed to delay surgery, as on her return from her pilgrimage there was no need for the planned operation, and she went on to become a Sacred Heart nun in Belgium.

15   **Clémentine Trouvé** was 14 when she was cured, having developed osteo-periostitis of the right foot. The doctor who saw her after her cure in the Baths certified that the scars had completely gone despite his earlier opinion that surgery was urgently needed; she became a Little Sister of the Assumption and featured in Emile Zola's novel, *Lourdes*.

16 and 17   **Marie Lermarchand** aged 18 and **Marie Lebranchu** came together on the French National Pilgrimage. These two cures are linked because both of them suffered from pulmonary tuberculosis and they were cured a day apart on 20 and 21 August 1892. They both returned to perfect health and Marie

Lebranchu went on to have eight children!

18 **Elisa Lesage** had a 'white tumour' (tuberculosis in the right knee) which in the nineteenth century was quite common among young people. At 18 years of age on 21 August 1892 she came to Lourdes and her cure occurred after she had visited the Baths; the Medical Bureau confirmed the cure that same day and 16 years later there were still no signs of a relapse.

19 **Sister Marie de la Présentation,** a Franciscan nun, was desperate to come to Lourdes. Those around her, including her doctor, knew that it was pointless trying to dissuade her. She had suffered from chronic gastroenteritis and tuberculosis for 12 years, and during the long train journey from Northern France she already began to feel a little better. While in Lourdes she was in the Rosary Basilica praying when a harsh stomach pain came over her, followed by the inexplicable disappearance of all her symptoms.

20 **Abbé Cirette** was born in 1847 and after a bad attack of influenza began to suffer from bouts of depression and mental confusion. No medication helped his situation and he became unable to walk normally, lost his speech, his memory and his independence. He joined a pilgrimage from Rouen to Lourdes in August 1893, and on arrival decided not to go straight to the Baths in case he took the place of a sick person. After lunch he felt a burning desire to go to the Grotto, and while there realized that he was no longer using his canes to walk. His cure was extremely sudden, and meant that he could return to his full pastoral duties as parish priest in Beaumontel.

21 **Aurélie Huprelle** was desperate as, at the young age of 26, she had lost all faith in medicine; for months she had suffered badly from pulmonary tuberculosis, and so against the advice of her doctors she joined the French National Pilgrimage to Lourdes in 1895. On arrival she was completely worn out by the journey but after getting off the train she was taken to the Baths. Immediately she felt she was cured and regained her zest for life. The subsequent investigation into her cure led to some doctors judging her illness to have been psychological, but finally the conclusion was reached that her cure had been sudden, complete and permanent.

22 **Esther Brachmann** was denied the ordinary life

of a young girl. Suffering from tuberculosis, she was incarcerated in hospital, and at the age of 15 joined the French National Pilgrimage. As soon as she came out of the Baths she was certain that she had been cured, and this proved to be so as on her return to the hospital in Villepinte the doctors were completely taken aback. In 1908, 12 years later, she was found still to be in perfect health.

23   **Jeanne Tulasne** had been in a bad way since Pott's Disease hit her spinal column leaving her with muscular atrophy, a club foot and an abscess on the back of her left thigh. When she was 20 she went to Lourdes with her diocesan pilgrimage, and while taking part in the Blessed Sacrament Procession, all of a sudden felt cured. The Medical Bureau and her doctors were able to confirm a lasting cure, which was authenticated ten years later.

24   **Clémentine Malot** had been suffering from progressive tuberculosis for more than five years. In 1898, when she was 25, she decided that she must go to Lourdes and she joined the French National Pilgrimage. It was a difficult journey, and on arrival she was taken to the Baths. The next morning she felt an improvement in her physical condition, and subsequently her cure was confirmed. Ten years later this was verified.

25   **Rose François** aged 36, had undergone unsuccessful surgery five times to rid her of lymphangitus in her right arm, and amputation was being recommended. Between the 20 and 22 August 1899 in Lourdes a complete transformation took place, as the infection completely cleared up and the wounds disappeared. On her return to Paris she regained normal use of her right hand, and her good health was sustained for years to come.

26   **Father Salvator** developed tuberculosis in his lungs in 1898 and two years later peritonitis set in. Determined to go to Lourdes, he arrived on 25 June 1900 at 7 p.m. and was taken straight to the Baths. Moments later he was completely rejuvenated, and there were no doubts from anyone witnessing the event that he had undergone a cure. He soon regained his appetite, and no signs of his former illness ever returned.

27   **Sister Maximilien** was a 43-year-old nun from the Sisters of Hope in Marseille who was suffering from a tumour on her liver. She had been ill for 15 years,

for five of which she was bedridden. The tumour which was eating away at her liver was incurable, and she had other complications. When she arrived in Lourdes on 21 May 1901 she was close to death, but within minutes of entering the Baths was back on her feet and completely cured. All the swellings in her body had disappeared.

28   **Marie Savoye** was in a very weak state of health when participating in the Blessed Sacrament Procession in Lourdes. For four of her 24 years she had suffered from acute rheumatic disease, and for the last 13 years her condition had deteriorated through heart disease. She was not even fit enough to be taken to the Baths. On 20 September 1901 during the Benediction of the Blessed Sacrament Procession all her symptoms suddenly disappeared, and on her return to normal life she helped others in gratitude for the help she had received during her long illness.

29   **Johanna Bezenac** was suffering not only from a serious form of pneumonia, which was the beginning of tuberculosis, but also a skin infection, which covered her face. She was ashamed to be seen in public. At the age of 28 she

came to Lourdes on her diocesan pilgrimage and during 8 and 9 August 1904 underwent a complete cure. This was attributed to the water from the spring and she returned home to Saint Laurent des Batons clear of all signs of illness.

30   **Sister Saint Hilaire** was in a sorry state when she came to Lourdes in August 1904. What had started as straightforward gastroenteritis had developed into an abdominal tumour resulting in a huge loss of weight and leaving her with virtually no skin on her back. Immediately she bathed in the Lourdes water she felt rejuvenated. Her appetite returned and she realized she had been cured. She frequently returned to Lourdes with the Rodez Pilgrimage in gratitude for her cure.

31   **Sister Sainte Béatrix** underwent two cures. When she came to Lourdes at the age of 42 suffering from probable tuberculosis she was transformed after her visit to the Baths. A year later she returned in thanks to the Virgin Mary, and this time her sight problems, which she had endured for 15 years, disappeared – also in the Baths.

32   **Marie-Thérèse Noblet** had spent much of her childhood quite seriously

ill, and in August 1904 when she was 14 years old she was diagnosed with Pott's Disease. A year later she came to Lourdes and on her return to the hospital after the Blessed Sacrament Procession she was cured. She later became a missionary in Papua New Guinea, founding the first order of indigenous nuns.

33 **Cécile Douville de Franssu** celebrated her 105th birthday on 26 December 1990. No one would have believed that she would reach this great age as when she was 19 tuberculosis peritonitis had been diagnosed following five years of illness, and an operation was considered essential. However, despite her very poor state of health, she insisted on going to Lourdes, and on 21 September 1905 she emerged from the Baths completely cured.

34 **Antonia Moulin** had already been to Lourdes once to no avail, and had returned home without any improvement to her health. Two years later, having spent six months in hospital with a benign tumour and abscess on her right leg, Antonia returned to Lourdes, a terminally ill 30-year-old. This time when she was taken to the Baths on 10 August 1907 it was found on removal of her dressings that

the wounds on her leg had healed 'like new'.

35 **Marie Borel** developed an abscess following an appendicitis operation, which would not heal, and more serious abscesses then appeared. She came to Lourdes with the French National Pilgrimage in August 1907, and when her dressing was changed on the evening of 21 August the lesions had healed. The next morning two more wounds were cured after a visit to the Baths.

36 **Virginie Haudebourg** wanted to make a pilgrimage to Lourdes in 1908 as it was the fiftieth anniversary of the Apparitions. She was 22 years old and life as a sick orphan had been hard. Now her illness was deemed incurable and terminal. During her second visit to Lourdes she experienced a violent pain during the Benediction of the Blessed Sacrament, and after an excellent night's sleep was found to be cured.

37 **Marie Biré** became blind after a serious illness. On 5 August 1908 she made a much longed-for pilgrimage to Lourdes. After Mass at the Grotto she completely recovered her sight, and to the doctors' amazement could even read the small print in the newspaper.

38   **Aimée Allope** had been unwell for ten years. At the age of 26 she had a kidney removed, but tuberculosis developed on her right side producing several enormous tumours. When she arrived in Lourdes she weighed just 44 kg (six-and-a-half stone), and her dressings had to be changed at least twice a day. At the age of 37 she was suddenly cured and this formerly sick person immediately gained weight and returned to normal life.

39   **Juliette Orion** could easily have given up when she was told there was no hope, and she wasn't even permitted to go to Lourdes. Instead, left on her own one night, she prayed to Our Lady of Lourdes and instantly felt a lot better, recovering both her voice and her appetite. Her doctor was called and after careful examination confirmed an unmistakeable cure.

40   **Marie Fabre** felt worn out by the age of 30. She was weakened by her three pregnancies, all of which were followed by difficult births, culminating in a uterine prolapse. In 1911 she requested to go to Lourdes and on her arrival could only attend the Blessed Sacrament Procession as she was too weak to go to the Baths or the Grotto. After the Benediction she felt much better, and stood up; by the time she returned to the Sept Douleurs Hospital she was asking for food, even though she had eaten nothing for two months. She returned home to lead a normal life.

41   **Henriette Bressolles** had been a military nurse during the First World War and in 1919 was admitted into hospital suffering from Pott's Disease. She was completely immobilized in a plaster cast. After attending the Blessed Sacrament Procession in Lourdes in 1924 she was taken to the Grotto. It was here that she was cured through what was described as a painful collapse. Her cure was finally recognized in 1957, and she died four years later at the age of 65.

42   **Lydia Brosse** lived to serve the sick in Lourdes for many years and finally died in 1984 at the age of 95. Until she was 41 she had suffered many problems with her bones, caused by tuberculosis resulting in unpleasant side effects. It was while returning from Lourdes in October 1930 that she discovered in herself the will and the strength to get up, all her wounds having healed. The doctors verified she was in 'blooming health'.

43   **Sister Marie Marguerite** was not expected

to live. The sisters of her Community had started a novena of prayers as she suffered kidney failure complicated by a series of heart attacks. On the last of the nine days of prayer she attended Mass, and suddenly felt a real easing of pain. Her swellings disappeared and she could walk. She was 100 kilometres from Lourdes but the miracle was nonetheless recognized.

44 **Louise Jamain** was an orphan and her mother and four brothers had all died from tuberculosis, which she had also suffered from for seven years. Against her doctor's advice she came to Lourdes on the Bernadette Pilgrimage in 1937. The journey exhausted her and she was given the last rites on 30 March. On 1 April she awoke and asked for something to eat. All her symptoms had gone, and she went on to marry and have two children.

45 **Francis Pascal** was three years and ten months old, and was blind and partly paralysed following meningitis. His family brought him to Lourdes in August 1938 and after visiting the Baths for a second time he regained his sight, and the paralysis disappeared. The doctors considered this a total and inexplicable medical cure

and Francis grew up to live a happy and healthy life.

46 **Gabrielle Clauzel** had been confined to bed for seven years suffering from rheumatic spondylitis. After Mass on 15 August 1943, she found she was able to get up and walk home on foot. She attributed her cure to praying to Our Lady of Lourdes, and this was verified by the Medical Bureau after the Second World War. She died at the age of 87 in 1982.

47 **Yvonne Fournier**'s arm was completely useless following an industrial accident, and during the next five and a half years she underwent nine operations. In 1945 Yvonne took part in the French National Pilgrimage and on 19 August after going to the Baths she regained all the normal feelings and complete mobility and strength was restored.

48 **Rose Martin** had spreading cervical cancer, which was inoperable. In 1947 she went to Lourdes and after her third visit to the Baths she was able to get up feeling no more pain. Once the effect of the massive dose of morphine she was taking had worn off, she knew that she was cured, and immediately regained her strength and weight.

49 Jeanne Gestas had continually suffered from digestive problems and at the age of 50 weighed a mere 44 kg (six and a half stone). During a visit to the Baths while on a pilgrimage in 1947 she felt an intense pain as though her intestines were being torn out. That afternoon she was much better, so the following morning returned to the Baths when she became certain of a cure. On her return home she immediately began to gain weight and normal life was resumed.

50 Marie-Thérèse Canin had spent ten years in hospital following the onset of Pott's Disease. With little strength left in her body, she arrived in Lourdes on 7 October 1947 and two days later during the Blessed Sacrament Procession she knew she was cured. Her appetite returned and now aged 37 she was able to resume a normal life.

51 Maddalena Carini had spent much of her childhood in hospital suffering from tuberculosis. Her health was slowly deteriorating and at 31 she weighed a pitiful 32 kg (five stone). She came to Lourdes and while in front of the Grotto began to feel better; she looked around to see if anyone had noticed. Apparently they had not, and so she decided not to say

anything until she was on the way home to Lomardie the following day.

52 Jeanne Frétel had spent much of her life in hospital, and her body was covered in scars from the many operations due to her tuberculosis peritonitis. In October 1948 she arrived in Lourdes heavily sedated with morphine and close to death. On the third day of her visit she attended a Mass for the sick at the St Bernadette Altar, and afterwards she began to feel better. When she could get up, walk and eat, the cure was complete and she was able to resume her career as a nurse.

53 Théa Angele aged 29 had lost all her faculties through multiple sclerosis, and following her supposed last wish to go to Lourdes, and after going to the Baths and attending the Blessed Sacrament Procession, she recovered completely. She regained her speech, ability to walk, muscular strength and appetite, and in 1955 entered the Convent of the Immaculate Conception in Lourdes.

54 Evasio Ganora had been diagnosed with Hodgkin's Disease and so, on 21 February 1949, with only a few months left to live, he went to Lourdes. He was taken in a wheelchair to the Baths and while immersed he felt a warm current flowing through his body. He was able to stand on his own and walk back to the hospital, and by the end of his pilgrimage he was able to help other sick people. Sadly he was run over by a tractor on his farm two years later.

55   Edeltraud Fulda's life changed dramatically when she was overcome by pain in her stomach and it was found that she had Addison's Disease. In August 1950 she went to Lourdes with her mother, where on arrival she was invited by a Dutch hospitalier to go to the Baths. She immediately felt better and was able to discontinue her daily hormone injections. She went on to make a complete recovery and was married on 16 April 1968.

56   Colonel Paul Pellegrin and his wife returned from Lourdes in October 1950, and the Colonel went to hospital for his usual quinine injections. He had been receiving treatment for an ulcer, which had appeared following an operation on his liver, and he had not been able to fight the infection. His wife had noticed after his visit to the Baths that her husband's wound had changed, and in fact the skin completely reformed in its place. His illness never returned.

57   Brother Léo Schwager astounded Professor Barbin from the faculty of medicine at Nantes University as he was suddenly cured of multiple sclerosis. After a sort of shock, similar to an electric shock, Brother Leo had been able to leave his wheelchair to kneel down to pray. He remained in good health for the rest of his life, and devoted much of his time to serving the sick in Lourdes.

58   Alice Couteault had multiple sclerosis and could no longer dress herself, with both her speech and sight being badly affected. She came to Lourdes in 1952 with enormous faith and trust that she might be cured, although her husband did not share this belief. After a visit to the Baths on 15 May, she found that she could walk, and a few hours later her speech returned. She was completely cured and returned to Lourdes many times as a nurse.

59   Marie Bigot suffered from arachnoiditid of posterior fossa leaving her unable to walk, speak or hear. She amazingly underwent three successive cures regaining all three faculties, the first being in 1953 and the other two a year later. She only ever returned to Lourdes to give thanks for her perfect health.

60 **Ginette Nouvel** had a rare incurable disease of the liver called Budd-Chiari Disease or hepatic vein thrombosis. She decided to make a pilgrimage to Lourdes in 1954 when she was 27 and followed all the celebrations. On her return home she found she no longer required any medical treatment and her life returned to normal. She died 16 years later from a medical error having suffered an intestinal perforation.

61 **Elisa Aloi** was 17 when she contracted tuberculosis on her right knee. In 1957 she went to Lourdes in despair as no treatment had helped. She returned home with no improvement, but the following year made a second visit to Lourdes where her dressings were applied with Lourdes water. On her return to Sicily, her doctor could not believe the result that her tumour had been completely cured, and she went on to marry and bring up a family of four children.

62 **Juliette Tamburini** had undergone 11 unsuccessful operations in as many years for a serious bone disease. She was in a bad way when she arrived in Lourdes in July 1959 on her diocesan pilgrimage. A complete cure followed an injection of Lourdes water into the fistula, but it was not until a year later that the Medical Bureau was informed, when it was found that the cure was instantaneous and medically inexplicable.

63 **Vittorio Micheli** was a young Alpine Hunter when he was diagnosed with a malignant tumour in his hip. When he went to Lourdes in 1963 he bathed in the Lourdes water and otherwise nothing notable took place. When he got home he was readmitted to the Military Hospital in Verona, and following a number of tests it was thought that the results were incorrectly interpreted. However, six months later Vittorio's bones had reformed, and he was once again in an excellent state of health.

64 **Serge Perrin** had been struck by hemiplegia, paralysis down one side of the body, and was in a very weak condition. During his second pilgrimage to Lourdes in 1970 he attended the Blessing of the Sick. Later that afternoon he discovered he could walk without crutches and that his sight had been restored. He left Lourdes a cured man and this was later confirmed by the doctors in 1978.

65 **Delizia Cirolli**'s parents were told that her leg would have to be amputated

because of a malignant tumour on her knee. They would not agree to this, and in 1976 when she was 12 years old she went on pilgrimage to Lourdes with her mother. There was no obvious change and by that Christmas her family and friends thought she was going to die; they prayed to Our Lady of Lourdes. Following a totally unexpected cure, Delizia returned to normal life, and is now married and the mother of three children.

66   **Jean-Pierre Bély** developed multiple sclerosis in 1972. His state of health deteriorated until he was totally incapacitated, and so in 1987 he went to Lourdes on the Rosary Pilgrimage. On the third day, after attending the Blessed Sacrament Procession, he felt a deep peace within him, and during the night a voice told him to get up and walk. So he did! Since then he has had perfect health.

The question often asked is: 'Why do pilgrims go to Lourdes, and do the sick hope for a miracle?' There are many reasons why people go on pilgrimage to Lourdes, and although relatively few miracles have taken place, there is so much to be gained from the experience. Frequently, pilgrims return home with a change of heart and a peace of mind. I well remember on one occasion in the days of going by train a very agitated lady accompanying her somewhat cross-looking husband who was in a wheelchair. A week later on the return journey she was a different person; no longer was she fussing around her husband all the time and an air of serenity had come over her. 'Do you know,' she explained, 'that my husband has smiled for the first time in years?'

Pilgrims go to Lourdes to help the sick, to follow the footsteps of Bernadette, to pray and process, and often simply to take a reflective week out of their otherwise hectic lives. Sick pilgrims have a holiday from their restricted environment at home, also giving their carers a much-needed break. People come for the support and friendship that going on pilgrimage offers, often concealing a deep-seated sadness in their own circumstances. Above all, going on pilgrimage puts all worries and concerns in perspective, enabling pilgrims to go home with a greater clarity of what is really important in their lives.

5

A Pilgrim's A–Z Guide to the Domaine

BATHS (PISCINES)

During the ninth apparition, Bernadette was asked by the Lady to drink at the spring and wash in the water at the grotto, although there was no spring to be seen. Bernadette scratched away at the surface of the earth, and found water rising which she was able to drink. Soon this spring was yielding 27,000 gallons of water a day (which has been maintained ever since, even in times of drought), and has been the site of some of the very earliest and most spectacular cures of Lourdes. The spring has been channelled into a reservoir from which the Baths are filled and there are also 35 drinking-fountain heads from which pilgrims can collect their own water. The extraordinary quality of this water is that it never becomes contaminated and can be kept for years.

Nearly half a million people visit the marble-clad Baths each year. It is the high point of many people's pilgrimage and can be a profoundly

moving, private, spiritual experience. Taking a bath may challenge the individual's need for comfort and dignity, but is a very visible and tangible demonstration of faith.

Each bath is a marble tank about three metres long. There are three steps down into the water, which is cold and about knee deep. Helpers from the Baths are in constant attendance to pray with the pilgrims and support them as they walk through the waters and sit down. The pilgrims are wrapped in a white cloth throughout as a recollection of their baptism.

'Go drink at the spring and bathe in its waters' is written in five languages over the entrances to the Baths.

The Baths are situated just beyond the Grotto. In 1862 the first wooden bathhouse was built in order that the sick could be immersed in the spring water; this was later replaced by a stone building. In 1954 the site of the Baths was moved to its present position where helpers and sick pilgrims alike are immersed in the waters.

There are five men's and ten women's baths plus two for children, with covered seating outside for while you wait. Leaflets are available in most languages which explain the process and meaning of taking a bath in Lourdes. Once at the head of the queue pilgrims are taken into one of the changing areas where they undress and are suitably covered in a cape or towel until entering the actual Bath area. It is advisable to arrive early in the morning to beat the crowds; everyone already waiting before the gates close will get a bath, but you can expect quite a long wait in the high season.

Opening Times

Open every day all the year round from 9 a.m. to 11 a.m. and from 2 p.m. to 4 p.m; Sundays from 2 p.m. to 4 p.m.

BLESSED SACRAMENT PROCESSION

During the thirteenth apparition the Lady told Bernadette to go to the priests and tell them to build a Chapel and let people come to this place in procession. On 4 April 1864 the ceremony that had been arranged for the inauguration of the statue of the Blessed Virgin Mary at the Grotto was the first major procession and commenced from the parish church in the old town. Over 10,000 people took part. This tradition soon became the heart of each day in Lourdes and from Easter until mid-October two ceremonies take place daily, one being the Blessed Sacrament Procession culminating in the Blessing of the Sick, and the other the Torchlight Procession (see page 49). The sacramental presence of Jesus in the form of bread and wine is the centre of the Catholic faith, and thereby acknowledge-ment of our need for the Bread of Life. This ceremony is the most important out of all the liturgical services in Lourdes, and its significance lies in its invitation to join with Christ through life's difficult journey.

Information

The Blessed Sacrament Procession starts in the Prairie just beyond St Bernadette's Church at 4.30 p.m. and moves through the Domaine past the Crowned Statue. For the last few years it has processed into the Basilica of St Pius X where Benediction takes place after the Blessing of the Sick; this change is due to the often intense heat in the afternoon in Rosary Square, where pilgrims used to assemble.

*Our Lady of Lourdes,
pray for us.*

BOLY MILL

Boly Mill, situated at 14,
Rue Bernadette Soubirous, is
Bernadette's birthplace and
is named after an English
doctor who lived there in the
seventeenth century (see
picture in colour photo
section); it is one of a
number of mills that were
situated on the fast-flowing
River Lapaca (this is
particularly well illustrated
at the Musée de le Petit
Lourdes; see page 54). Aged
34, François Soubirous came
to help Claire Castérot, a
young widow whose
husband had been killed in
a cart accident, to run the
mill. He fell in love with the
younger daughter Louise
and on 19 November 1842
they were married in a civil
ceremony as they were in
mourning for François'
mother who had just died.
A church wedding followed
on 7 January 1843. Four of
their five children were born
and raised here, but François
was no businessman
allowing his customers to
pay on credit and so in 1852
the mill was sold. Although
the new owner worked
the mill for himself the
Soubirous family were able
to continue living here, but
when François was unable to
find work and could not pay
the rent the family briefly
lived at Rives House and

then moved to the Cachot
(see below).

The mill has been turned
into a museum depicting
what the rooms would have
looked like during the
Soubirous family's
occupation.

Opening Times

Open 1 April to 30 October
from 9 a.m. to 12 p.m. and
from 2 p.m. to 6.30 p.m. Open
31 October to 31 March from
9 a.m. to 12 p.m. and from
3 p.m. to 5 p.m. Admission free.

BRANCARDIERS AND HANDMAIDS

The word brancardier
means stretcher-bearer, and
in Lourdes the men wearing
leather or canvas bratelles
(or straps) indicate that they
are specifically there to help
carry and care for the sick,
and also to marshal public
events. The lady helpers,
traditionally known as
handmaids, are normally
identifiable as they wear
some form of uniform
according to their
pilgrimage, often similar to
that of a nurse.

*Christ has no other hands
but yours to do his work
today.*

THE CACHOT

This is the former prison and
home to the Soubirous
family from June 1856 to
autumn 1858 after their

enforced departure from Boly Mill (see picture in colour photo section). From here they all desperately tried to scrape a living: François became a labourer; Louise a cleaning-woman; and the children collected scraps to sell to the rag-and-bone man. Situated at 15, Rue des Petits Fossés, just off the Rue de la Grotte up the hill towards the Old Town, the Cachot – now a museum – is an essential place for pilgrims to visit. The cell remains as it was in 1848, with just a stone sink and small fireplace and one or two souvenirs including Bernadette's sock and a pair of clogs. It is heart-rending to see the humble conditions in which the family lived and from where these extraordinary events took place. Mass is celebrated here for small groups of pilgrims by arrangement.

Opening Times

Open 1 April to 31 October from 9.00 a.m. to 12 p.m. and from 2.00 p.m. to 7.00 p.m. Open 1 November to 31 March from 3 p.m. to 5.00 p.m. Admission free.

'I am the Light of the World.'

CANDLES

Lighting a candle as a prayer to remember loved ones is a strong tradition in the Catholic Church, and in Lourdes this tradition is particularly prevalent. Candles with paper-holders – on which are printed hymns and prayers used in the Torchlight Procession (see page 49) – can be purchased in any of the numerous shops. Between the Grotto and the Baths, just to the left of the water fountains, are impressive votive stands for which many different sized candles can be bought for pilgrims to light themselves (see picture in black and white photo section); it is also possible to leave a candle with your intentions in the Grotto to be lit at a later date.

As I place this light by the rock, let my life be filled with your light.

CITÉ SECOURS ST PIERRE (CITY OF THE POOR)

This organization welcomes pilgrims who would not otherwise be able to afford to come to Lourdes. It was set up in 1956, and is a 20-minute steep walk from the Domaine, situated in Avenue Monseigneur Rodhain. It is run and organized by 24 salaried staff, four seasonal workers, three nuns and a chaplain, and 100 volunteers at any one time. Guests here are supported by the generosity of other pilgrims contributing what they can afford themselves, and are expected to help with the day-to-day running of the centre; pilgrims must be at least 18 years of age and volunteer for a minimum of three weeks. It is open all the year round and accommodates 500 pilgrims. Just above the Cité is a beautiful natural small amphitheatre under the trees with an imposing altar where Mass is celebrated for pilgrimages by prior arrangement.

Information

Tel: + 33 (0) 5 62 42 71 11.
Fax: + 33 (0) 5 62 42 71 19.

CROWNED VIRGIN

This statue is situated between Rosary Square and the Esplanade and is the symbol of Marian devotion for every pilgrim in Lourdes (see picture in black and white photo section). It commemorates the ceremony of the coronation of Our Lady of Lourdes on 3 July 1876, and is a popular meeting point for pilgrims, in particular day pilgrims. The bronze statue is 2.5 metres high and stands on a granite pedestal. The Crowned Virgin is holding a set of rosary beads containing six decades (as opposed to the normal five). Fresh flowers are placed all around the foot of the statue, and there is a tradition for pilgrims to leave a flower as a prayer that they will return to

Lourdes another year. (A flower kiosk can be found outside St Joseph's Gate.)

DAY PILGRIMS

Pilgrims visiting Lourdes for one day are well catered for as from 1 July to 30 September there is a special programme arranged each day. The whole day programme includes a celebration of Mass; the Way of the Cross; a guided tour of places associated with Bernadette; the Blessed Sacrament Procession and the Torchlight Procession. Booking is not necessary, but do check the notice board at the Forum Information for any changes.

Information

Meet at the Crowned Virgin at either 8.30 a.m. or 2.15 p.m., where you will be put in different groups according to language and led by a priest. There will be someone to welcome you carrying a green placard marked 'Day Pilgrims'. Services for day pilgrims take place in the Chapel Saint Cosmas and Damien in the Acceuil Jean-Paul II. Mass in English is said here at 9 a.m. every day, including Sunday, followed by a short introduction to Lourdes.

DOMAINE

This is the centre-point of Lourdes, which encases the Shrine and all the major sites that pilgrims head for on their arrival. Between 1861 and 1864 Monseigneur Bertrand Laurence purchased the surrounding land around the Massabielle Grotto; in 1869 the site of the Way of the Cross on the Espelugues Hill was added. Later on, between 1874 and 1942, the Prairie on the right-hand side (north bank) of the River Gave was gradually acquired.

The Domaine is a sacred area where silence is requested and pilgrims are asked to be suitably clad. The main gate is St Joseph's Gate, but access is also possible through the Lacets Gate, Upper Gate, Meadow Gate, St Michael's Gate, Boissarie Gate and Forest Gate. The whole area covers 50 hectares (120 acres) and is one of the largest shrines in the world. It comes under the authority of the Bishop of Tarbes and Lourdes, and the Shrine itself is run by the Rector of the Sanctuaries and his Chaplains. The gates close at midnight and open at 5.00 a.m.; however, outside these hours you can enter or go out via the Lacets Gate, just between the Grotto and candle votive stands. This path comes out on Avenue Monseigneur Theas up the hill just beyond the Basilicas.

THE ESPLANADE

This is just over one kilometre long (1,100 yards) and is the main avenue in the Domaine. It is the route followed each day by the Processions. At one end near St Michael's Gate is the Breton Calvary Cross and at the other end the statue of the Crowned Virgin. To the south the pilgrim can just make out the slightly domed grass covering of the St Pius X Underground Basilica.

FORUM INFORMATION

A rotunda-shaped building marked 'Forum Information' is situated just inside St Joseph's Gate. It is vital to check details of all daily events here on the noticeboards which are posted at about 6.00 p.m. every day. Audio-guides are also available from the kiosk to the front of the centre; these cost 5 Euros.

Opening Times

April to October open every day, including Sunday, from 8.30 a.m. to 12.15 p.m. and from 1.45 p.m. to 6.30 p.m. (NB July and August open all day). November to March open from 9.00 a.m. to 12 p.m. and from 2.00 p.m. to 6.00 p.m.

GROTTO

Nestling under the overhang of the huge Basilicas is the

41

Grotto, the heart of the Lourdes Shrine, where the Apparitions of 1858 took place (see picture in colour photo section). The statue of Our Lady, carved by Joseph Fabisch of Lyons, clearly marks the spot where Bernadette saw her Lady surrounded by light (see picture in black and white photo section). The Massabielle (or old rock) provides an impressive background to such a sacred place. To the rear of the cave is the spring that Bernadette found with her bare hands by scratching away at the surface of the earth; it is now covered with a glass screen and clear for all to see, and supplies the drinking fountains and the Baths. To the right of the Grotto is a rose bush, which acts as a reminder that the parish priest of Lourdes, Father Peyramale, requested that a rose should bloom in February as a sign of the authenticity of Bernadette's story. There are two paving stones in front of the Grotto: one marks the place where Bernadette was standing during the first Apparition – 'Place ou Priait'; the other marks the ancient course of the Savy Millstream, now covered over, which at that time flowed between the River Gave and the Grotto (see picture in black and white photo section).

This supremely holy forecourt is where pilgrims come in silent prayer, and where three million candles are lit as a symbol of faith. A new altar taken from a natural piece of stone was erected on Maundy Thursday, 2004, and each day Masses are celebrated by pilgrimages from all over the world.

Pilgrims can walk round through the back of the Grotto, and it is traditional to either touch or kiss the rock. There is a box for personal petitions behind the altar to the right.

Information

For times and languages of Masses refer to the noticeboard outside the Forum.

> *Prayer for the Grotto*
> *Mary, Mother of Jesus,*
> *through you we thank*
> *God for bringing us*
> *safely to Lourdes. Help*
> *us to spend a few hours*
> *each day in prayer and*
> *penance. Teach us to love*
> *God and our neighbours,*
> *and give us the strength*
> *to do what is your will*
> *while we are here. Grant*
> *us, and all those we pray*
> *for, the graces and*
> *favours which you know*
> *will be for the goodness*
> *of us all. Our Lady of*
> *Lourdes, pray for us.*
> *Saint Bernadette, pray*
> *for us.*

HEMICYCLE

This is the building attached to the Church of St Bernadette which hosts the French Conference of Bishops in the autumn; it houses 500 people and is used mainly for conferences.

HOSPITALITÉ OF OUR LADY OF LOURDES

This organization is based in the newly furbished Accueil Jean-Paul II alongside the Esplanade facing St Michael's Gate on the left-hand side. It is the organization responsible for the day-to-day running of Lourdes, and it works in liaison with groups who wish to bring pilgrimages to Lourdes. It undertakes to supervise the safe arrival of sick pilgrims, and to serve as marshals at all the main ceremonies. Under its auspices it is possible to come as a Stagier, staying in simple accommodation and working for the benefit of the whole of Lourdes in whatever capacity is required. Members of the Hospitalité undertake a spirit of service, always putting the interest of others before their own, and must be available to be relied on when people are in need, within their service to Lourdes.

Information

Tel: +33 (0) 5 62 42 80 80.
Fax: +33 (0) 5 62 42 80 81.

E-mail: hospitalite@lourdes-france.com

INFORMATION BUREAU

See Forum Information, page 41.

LIBRAIRE

The library is just to the right of the information centre as you go into the Domaine through St Joseph's Gate. This is not a lending library, but sells relevant books on Lourdes and Bernadette along with other religious books. Videos, CDs, tapes and postcards are also available.

Opening Times

Open every day from 8.30 a.m. to 12.30 p.m. and from 1.30 p.m. to 6.30 p.m.

MAGAZINE

The *Lourdes Magazine*, available from the Libraire and kiosks around the Domaine, is a monthly publication in six languages giving useful current information and interesting and informative articles on the various facets of Lourdes; it also lists the pilgrimages currently in Lourdes. Annual subscription for eight issues is available for 25 Euros; magazines are priced individually at 3.80 Euros. Forms for subscription are in each magazine. Past editions are also for sale.

PRAIRIE

On the other side of the River Gave from the Grotto is the beautifully laid out Prairie (see picture in black and white photo section), which is an ideal place to get away from the crowds of the Domaine. The Tent of the Adoration of the Eucharist, where the Blessed Sacrament is kept at all times, is a perfect place for private prayer. A French Mass is celebrated here at 8 a.m. every day. Just beyond here, along the river bank, is a short 'water walk', which provides eight water fountains, each set in a little flower garden.

The Prairie is also used for open-air Masses and special events, weather permitting, and there have been as many as 300,000 pilgrims congregated here. An alternative Way of the Cross for those who are unable to manage the Espelugues Hill Stations runs along the right-hand bank of the River Gave, near the bridge.

ROSARY SQUARE

This is the forecourt between the Crowned Virgin statue and the Basilicas, with ramps either side that lead up to the Crypt and Upper Basilica; it is where the Torchlight Procession concludes (see picture in black and white photo section). There are also celebrations of Mass that take place here, particularly on Palm Sunday and at the end of the Rosary Pilgrimage. Almost 40,000 people can be accommodated in this square, and on either side trees have been planted to provide some shade.

SHRINES AND CHURCHES

Situated in Rosary Square, the Rosary Basilica and the Basilica of the Immaculate Conception (or Upper Basilica) dominate the Domaine and provide a backcloth to many important celebrations in Lourdes.

The imposing statues situated at intervals on the ramparts overlooking Rosary Square are the saints who welcome us to Lourdes, and who are worthy of a closer look: St Remy, Bishop of Reims in the fifth century, is portrayed receiving a dove sent from heaven (see picture in black and white photo section); St Vincent de Paul founded the Vincentians and the Daughters of Charity in the seventeenth century and is remembered as a benefactor of all those who are abandoned by society; St Joachim, father of the Blessed Virgin, carries a basket with two doves as a reminder of the offering he made when Mary was presented in the Temple in Jerusalem; St Bernards a prominent eleventh-century abbot, holds his crozier and is the patron saint of St Bernadette; St John the Baptist holds a cross in his left hand, his right hand points to the true Lamb of God; St John the Evangelist holds a pen in one hand and a book in the other signifying the importance of his writings in the scriptures; St Hyacinth, a Polish saint, has a ciborium in one hand and a statue of the Blessed Virgin in the other showing his special devotion to the Eucharist; St Anne, the mother of Our Lady, is shown teaching the scriptures to her daughter; St Louis-Marie Grignon de Montfort, canonized in 1947, is holding the Crucified Jesus, having based his spiritual teaching on Our Lady and the Cross; St Martin, Bishop of Tours, holds his hands up towards heaven in prayer; St Roch (pronounced rock) fittingly takes his place as patron saint of the sick; St Thérèse of Lisieux, carved by a Trappist monk, Brother Marie-Bernard, holds the Gospels in her hand, and is depicted teaching the meaning of truth and holiness; and St Bernadette is resting on a stone, sheep sitting at her feet while she recites the Rosary. The Salus Infirmorum is the fine monument on the left of the main pathway from St Joseph's Gate, and was erected by the Diocese of Cambrai in 1912.

The original Crypt was built dramatically into the Massabielle rock over the Grotto, with the Upper Basilica constructed soon afterwards when the Crypt became too small for the demand from pilgrims; 30 years later the Rosary Basilica was built.

The Crypt

The Crypt, designed and constructed by the architect Hippolyte Durand, was started in 1863 and the first Mass celebrated on 19 May 1866 by the then Bishop of Tarbes Monseigneur Bertrand Laurence in the presence of Bernadette herself. It is dedicated to the Adoration of the Blessed Sacrament, and so it is fitting that the Host is exposed all day in a monstrance presented by Pope John Paul II in 1983 during his pilgrimage to Lourdes. On either side of the altar are four chapels; these are dedicated to the Sacred Heart, St Peter, St Joseph and St John the Evangelist. Above the altar is Joseph Fabisch's 1868 sculpture of the Madonna and Child. This first response to the Lady's request 'Let a chapel be built' was soon too small for the demand and in 1866 work was started on the Basilica of the Immaculate Conception (see pictures in colour and black and white photo sections). The Crypt is now a quiet place for private prayer.

The Basilica of the Immaculate Conception (or Upper Basilica)

The Upper Basilica was consecrated on 2 July 1876 although completed in 1871, and was also designed by Monsieur Durand (see picture in black and white photo section); in 1874 it was raised to the status of a minor Basilica by the Pope and the tympanum above the main portal bears the image of Pius IX. The Chapel of St Germaine and the Chapel of St Bertrand contain marble plaques, one with the text used by Monseigneur Bertrand Laurence when he officially recognized the Apparitions as authentic, and the other the dates of the 18 Apparitions engraved with the words spoken by Our Lady. The altar is situated directly above the spot where the Apparitions took place in the Grotto, and on every hour the four main bells play the refrain to the Lourdes hymn, 'Ave Maria'.

A significant feature of this building is the stained glass. The windows in the side chapels recall the story of the Apparitions in Lourdes in 1858 and their recognition by Monseigneur Laurence

through to the consecration of the Basilica and the crowning of the Statue of Our Lady of Lourdes. They were designed and made by Laurent Gsell. A statue of the Crowned Virgin by Emilien Cabuchet stands at the entrance of the choir, and was commissioned to commemorate the coronation of Our Lady of Lourdes in 1876. Behind the high altar are five more chapels dedicated to Our Lady of the Rosary, Our Lady of La Salette, Our Lady of Victories, Our Lady of Mount Carmel and Our Lady of Pontmain.

The stained-glass windows in the nave illustrate scenes from the Old Testament on the left side, and Mary and her importance in the history of the Church on the right. In the centre the tenth window represents the Trinity. The Old Testament windows show the fall of Adam and Eve, the vision of the Lady crowned with 12 stars, Noah's Ark, Abraham sacrificing his son Isaac, Moses and the burning bush, King David playing his harp, Judith who freed Israel from the Assyrians, the coronation of Esther, and finally Anne and Joachim, the parents of Our Lady. The nine windows on the right-hand side show the story of the Immaculate Conception with the Annunciation of Our Lady and follow the debate of the Church elders through to Pope Pius IV's acceptance of the Dogma in 1854.

Information

Wheelchair access is through the door on Avenue Monseigneur Theas.

The Rosary Basilica

This was designed by the architect Leopold Harvey and constructed 30 years after the Apparitions (see picture in black and white photo section). Built in the neo-Byzantine style, its three naves are laid out in the shape of a Greek Cross, the arms of the cross being the same length. It was opened in 1889 and consecrated two years later, providing a church that can accommodate 2,000 pilgrims. It is linked to the front of the Crypt and Upper Basilica with two impressive ramps of stonework either side representing two great arms of welcome and leading up to the entrance forecourt; here its dome bears a cross within a gold crown to commemorate the ceremony of the coronation of Our Lady of Lourdes (see picture in colour photo section). Within the Romanesque doorway is Maniglier's handsome sculpture of Our Lady holding the infant Jesus bestowing a rosary to St Dominic, promoter of the Rosary in the thirteenth

century (see picture in black and white photo section).

Once inside the Rosary Basilica the open arms of Our Lady of Lourdes welcome pilgrims in the form of a painting by Edgar Maxence made in 1920 on the vaulted ceiling of the choir. Inscribed in gold are the words 'To Jesus through Mary', written by the Bishop of Tarbes and Lourdes when the mosaic was blessed on 15 August 1920. Within the 15 side chapels are the Mysteries of the Rosary represented in beautiful mosaics produced by Facchina in Paris from 1895 to 1907. The five Joyful Mysteries are in the South Transept, the five Glorious Mysteries in the north transept and the five Sorrowful Mysteries in the apse behind the high altar. The Joyful Mysteries start with the Annunciation, then the Visitation, followed by the Birth of Jesus, the Presentation in the Temple, and the Finding of Jesus in the Temple. The Sorrowful Mysteries are linked with the Passion and death of Jesus and show the Agony of Jesus in the Garden of Gethsemane, the Scourging at the Pillar, the Crowning with Thorns, the Carrying of the Cross, and the Crucifixion. The Glorious Mysteries are the Resurrection of Jesus, the Ascension, the Descent of the

47

Holy Spirit, the Assumption of Our Lady into Heaven and the Coronation of Our Lady.

True to its name the Rosary Basilica is a popular place either for individuals or small groups of pilgrims to meditate the Rosary. (See page 65 for meditation on the Rosary.)

Information

Check the noticeboards outside the Forum Information for times and languages of Masses.

The Chapel of St Bernadette

The Chapel of St Bernadette (not to be confused with St Bernadette's Church) stands to the left of the Rosary Basilica. It is decorated with a mosaic of Our Lady of Lourdes surrounded by angels, and is situated between two other chapels: the one on the left dedicated to St Paschal Baylon and the one on the right dedicated to Our Lady of Guadalupe. Services for the sick and celebration of the Eucharist are conducted here, weather permitting.

The Basilica of St Pius X (Underground Basilica)

In 1956, ready to commemorate the centenary of the Apparitions, this huge underground Basilica was built to accommodate the ever-increasing number of pilgrims coming to Lourdes. It was consecrated by the future Pope John XXIII on 25 March 1958, exactly 100 years to the day of the sixteenth Apparition when Our Lady revealed to Bernadette, 'I am the Immaculate Conception'.

The Basilica is constructed in the shape of an upside-down boat and made entirely of reinforced concrete supported by 58 triangular posts forming 29 porticos (see picture in colour photo section). This design was the work of three architects – Pierre Pinsard, Andre Le Donnet and Pierre Vago – and ensures maximum visibility of the central altar from wherever you are seated; television screens have also been installed for this purpose. Being 12,000 square metres, it is one of the largest buildings in the world, holding 25,000 pilgrims. There is some seating, but much of the space is for the use of voitures and wheelchairs, with easy access through wide ramps situated round the building.

From April to October an International Mass is concelebrated at 9 a.m. on Wednesdays and Sundays. This celebration is attended by pilgrims from all over the world, and illustrates the wideness of the Christian

Church, particularly within Lourdes.

The raised walkway round the inside of the Basilica contains both the Stations of the Cross and the Mysteries of the Rosary. The 18 Apparitions are illustrated in illuminated stained glass by Margotton, Falcucci, Solere and Loir; also included are 34 images of saints and martyrs from all over the world with a short biography of each one attached to the adjacent pillar. A small altar at the east end provides a more intimate setting for smaller gatherings of pilgrims to celebrate Mass.

St Bernadette's Church

This is on the other side of the River Gave from the Grotto almost on the exact spot where Bernadette met Our Lady on 16 July 1858, because the Grotto had been barricaded off by the police (see picture in colour photo section); this church was built in 1986 and dedicated two years later on the Feast of the Annunciation, 25 March 1988. Designed by the architect Jean-Paul Felix, it was built in the shape of a semi-circular amphitheatre. It can hold up to 5,000 pilgrims, and can be divided into two by a partition. There are eight adjacent rooms which are used for smaller groups of pilgrims.

Information

For times and languages of Masses in all five churches, consult the noticeboards outside the Forum Information. There is an International Youth Mass here every Saturday at 8.15 p.m. from the first Saturday in July to the first Saturday in September.

St Joseph's Chapel

This is a small chapel built partly underground just off the Esplanade near St Michael's Gate. It is mainly used for private gatherings and holds about 450 pilgrims.

TORCHLIGHT PROCESSION

The torchlight procession is the culmination point of each day in Lourdes, which commences at 8.45 p.m. from near the Grotto. Here is where pilgrims are brought together by the simple message from Our Lady to Bernadette, 'Let the people come to this place in procession'. It is a moving experience to see so many pilgrims from all the corners of the earth gathering in one accord, many following their pilgrimage banner and holding their candles in faith as prayers are led over the public address system, with everyone joining in their own tongue in singing the Lourdes hymn.

The procession slowly wends its way round the Esplanade until it congregates in Rosary Square in front of the Basilicas. Here the ceremony is concluded with the singing of 'Salve, Regina' (see page 80), prayers and Benediction, after which pilgrims quietly disperse. Individual pilgrims are welcome to join in by standing on the ramps either side of the Basilica.

VOITURES

A prominent feature within Lourdes are the many voitures which are used for the transportation of sick pilgrims around the sanctuaries (see picture in black and white photo section). They give protection both against the sun and the rain with their large canvas hoods, and provide a comfortable mode of transport for those unable to walk very far.

Information

Voitures can be hired from the Acceuil Marie Saint Frai Hospital (see page 56).

WATER

The very special characteristic of Lourdes water is that it never becomes contaminated and can be kept for years. Containers of all shapes and sizes can be purchased in any of the shops outside the Domaine and pilgrims can collect water to take home from one of the 35 fountain heads just to the left of the Grotto. Many pilgrims wash themselves from these taps, as an alternative to going in the Baths. The water itself has been scientifically tested, and no extraordinary qualities have been found.

THE WAY OF THE CROSS

Continuing on as part of the whole Massabielle feature are the life-size Stations of the Cross (see pictures in colour photo section), an important penitential act in the life of a Christian, following the Passion, death and resurrection of Christ (for Stations of the Cross, see page 71). Just inside the entrance is a memorial, the Moulins Monument, erected in memory of 33 French pilgrims from the Diocese of Moulins who died in a train accident in 1922.

The first Station of the Cross stands just outside the upper gate to the Rosary Basilica in Avenue Monseigneur Theas. They are all made in cast-iron and overlaid with bronze, and were inaugurated on 14 September 1912. You will also see here a huge cross standing 12 metres high which was a gift from the Diocese of Beauvais. Most of the tableaux have been gifts from French dioceses, along with a few give by pilgrimages from other countries.

At the first Station are the Holy Steps, Scala Sancta, where some pilgrims choose to mount the stairs on their knees as a sign of penance. The Way of the Cross winds round this hillside above the Basilicas for nearly a mile to the Calvary. Prehistoric remains have been found at the top in the Espelugues Cave.

A fifteenth Station has been added in the form of a large circular stone embossed with sun rays leaning against a rock, to remind pilgrims of Christ's tomb after the stone had been rolled away.

Information

Although it is possible to take a wheelchair round the Way of the Cross, the ground is rough and hard-going, and it is not recommended. An alternative way can be found in the Prairie (see page 44).

'He is risen as he promised, Alleluia!'

6

Other Places of Interest in and Around Lourdes

BARTRÈS

Bartrès is a small village situated four kilometres from Lourdes, where Bernadette lived for two periods of her life. The first time was in November 1844 when she was ten months old. Her mother, Louise, could no longer feed Bernadette following an accident with a candle which burnt her breast, so she was sent to a wet nurse, Marie Laguës, whose 13-day-old baby had just died. Bernadette's second visit came when the Soubirous family were in a state of destitution following their arrival at the Cachot. It was decided that she should return to Marie Laguës and work on the farm as a shepherdess and help in the house. Bernadette still could not read or write and so in the evening Marie Laguës tried to teach her the Catechism; however, she became so homesick that she returned to her family in January 1858.

There are still reminders of Bernadette's time in Bartrès.

The shepherd's hut or sheepfold where she looked after the sheep remains unchanged, and can be found up a rocky path which opens into a meadow. Burg House, in the middle of Bartrès, is a handsome farmhouse, and it is here that Bernadette lived with her foster mother, Marie Laguës. This has been restored after a fire, and the kitchen is just as it would have been in the middle of the nineteenth century.

The Church of St John the Baptist dates to the end of the fourteenth century. Parts of the church have changed considerably over the years, and it has even been used as a refuge. The altar dates from the seventeenth century, and behind it is a triptych showing scenes of the life of John the Baptist. Marie Laguës is buried in the churchyard.

CASTLE FORTRESS

The Castle Fortress is situated in 25, Rue du Fort, off Rue de la Grotte.

Standing on a hill in a prominent position overlooking the town on both sides, the Castle Fortress begs a visit (see picture in colour photo section). There are steps up from the Place du Fort, and the Rampe du Fort provides the return journey. There is also a lift at the ticket entrance on Rue du Fort, with a café opposite. The castle has had a long history since Roman times, but the existing building dates mainly from the seventeenth and eighteenth centuries, with a fourteenth-century keep; among other uses it was once a state prison and also the residence of the Counts of Bigorre.

In 1920 a museum was opened in the Castle, housing many treasures mainly associated with Pyrenean customs including traditional costumes, tools and artefacts. On Bastille Day, every 14 July, there is a magnificent firework display from the Castle.

Opening Times and Information

Open from 1 April to 30 September from 9 a.m. to 12 p.m. and from 1.30 p.m. to 6 p.m. Open from 1 October to 31 March from 9 a.m. to 12 p.m. and from 2 p.m. to 6 p.m. (Friday 5 p.m.). Closed on Tuesdays.) Disabled facilities. Adults 5 Euros; children aged 6 to 12 years 2.50 Euros.

MUSEUMS

Within the Domaine just inside St Michael's Gate at the end of the Esplanade is a small covered Diorama with nine attractive tableaux scenes taken from the life of Bernadette.

Information

Entrance free. Always open as there is no doorway.

Musée Grévin

This waxwork museum is run by the famous waxwork museum in Paris with 125 lifesize figures. The ground floor is devoted to illustrations of the events in Bernadette's life, and the upper floors depict the life of Christ. There is an impressive tableau based on Leonardo da Vinci's *Last Supper*. In 1993 a reproduction of the glass casket in which Bernadette lies at Nevers was added.

Information

87, Rue de la Grotte. Open from 1 April to 31 October from 9 a.m. to 11.40 a.m. and from 1.30 p.m. to 6.30 p.m. Sundays open from 10 a.m. to 11.40 a.m. and from 1.30 p.m. to 6.30 p.m. Adults 5.50 Euros; children aged 6 to 12 years 2.75 Euros.

Musée de la Nativité (Museum of the Nativity)

This depicts the story of Jesus' childhood in 14 tableaux, including scenes from the Nativity and the flight into Egypt. There is a scale model of life in Palestine at the time Jesus lived.

Information

21, Quai Saint Jean. Open daily from 1 April to 31 October from 9 a.m. to 12 p.m. and from 1.30 p.m. to 7 p.m. Adults 5 Euros; children aged 6 to 12 years 2.50 Euros.

Musée de Lourdes

This describes the history of Lourdes as it was in 1858. Here is an opportunity to see the skilled crafts produced in the nineteenth century, what the shops had to sell and the costumes worn, and absorb the atmosphere of the time of the Apparitions.

Information

Rue de l'Egalité (next to the cemetery). Open daily from 1 April to 31 October from 9 a.m. to 11.45 a.m. and from 1.30 p.m. to 6.45 p.m. Adults 5 Euros; children aged 6 to 12 years 2.50 Euros.

Musée de le Petit Lourdes

This is an open-air museum of a miniature version of Lourdes on a scale of 1 : 20, showing all the main buildings of Lourdes in 1858 set in a lovely garden. It is particularly helpful in showing how the little brook (now covered over) that Bernadette crossed flowed between the Grotto and the River Gave, and also how many mills were worked on the fast-flowing River Lapaca at that time.

Information

68, Avenue Peyramale. Open daily from 1 April to 30 June and from 1 September to 20 October from 9 a.m. to 12 p.m. and from 1.30 p.m. to 7 p.m. July and August open from 9 a.m. to 7 p.m. Adults 5 Euros; children aged 6 to 12 years 2.50 Euros.

Old Presbytery

Old Presbytery, 7 Chaussée Maransin. The exterior of this building remains as it was in 1858, but has now become a public lending library. It played an important role during the Apparitions as it was here that Bernadette came to deliver the messages from Our Lady to the priests. Part of the wall from the garden and the door through which Bernadette entered have been conserved, and a plaque commemorates the events.

Parish Church

The original Parish church that Bernadette attended was

destroyed by fire in 1905. Construction of a new church had in fact been started in 1875, and is situated off Rue St Pierre near the Tourist Information Office (see picture in colour photo section). An important relic inside is the stone baptismal font, saved from the old church, in which Bernadette was christened in 1844. There is also a statue of the Madonna and Child, and the confessional of Father Peyramale, parish priest at the time of the Apparitions. His tomb lies beneath the church in the crypt.

Cafés

An essential part of the pilgrim's day in Lourdes is a visit to one of the many street cafés where people come together to relax and exchange experiences. Most provide a simple meal along with a large range of both alcoholic and non-alcoholic beverages. During the season they are open all day and until quite late at night.

Lac de Lourdes

The lake is signposted from the N640 Pau Road. A large café offering a simple menu is situated at the side of this lake where there are small boats for hire. It is worth taking the short taxi-ride to come and relax by the waterside in this beautiful setting. Near by is an 18-hole golf course.

Information

Open during the season (1 April to 31 October).

Cemetery

The Cemetery is situated in Rue de l'Egalité. Here is the tomb of the Soubirous family, although Bernadette herself is encased in a glass reliquary at Nevers. The most recent member of the family to be buried here was Bernard Soubirous in 2002.

Cinema

The Cinema is situated at 6, Avenue Monseigneur Schoepfer, and shows two films, *Bernadette* and *The Passion of Bernadette*, in six languages: French, Italian, English, Dutch, German and Spanish.

Information

For times of showing, see listings in the window. Air conditioned.

Hospice

The Hospice is located next to the Municipal Hospital, 3, Avenue Alexandre Marqui. This was the Convent of the Sisters of Nevers where they ran a school and hospital, and it is where Bernadette lived during the eight years after the Apparitions until she joined the order in Nevers as a nun. It is here that she made her First Communion, and pilgrims can view the

Oratory and the Old Parlour which houses a few souvenirs of when she lived there.

Hospitals

There are two residential, hospice-style hospitals for the use of sick and disabled pilgrims, either on their own or within an organized group.

Accueil Notre-Dame (within the Domaine)
Tel: +33 (0) 5 62 42 80 61.
Fax: +33 (0) 5 62 42 79 48.
E-mail: *and-lourdes@ Lourdes-france.com*
Accueil Marie St Frai (formerly known as the Sept Douleurs – the Seven Sorrows of Our Lady, *Rue Marie St Frai*
Tel: +33 (0) 5 62 42 80 00.
Fax: +33 (0) 5 62 42 80 02.
E-mail: accueil.Saint-Frai@wanadoo.fr

Lift

To avoid the steep gradient of the Rue de la Grotte a municipal lift has been installed which takes wheelchairs. Go over Pont Vieux, turn right and take an immediate left into Rue de l'Arberet. On the left is a no-through road, at the end of which is the lift which takes you up to Rue de l'Egalité just below the cemetery. This lift helps ease the climb up the hill by about 80%.

Pic du Jer Funicular Railway

The Pic du Jer Funicular Railway is situated in 59, Avenue Francis Lagardere. The best way to take this trip is to join the Little Train on a circular ticket from outside St Joseph's Gate which you can hop off and re-alight at any of its six stops (see below). The funicular railway runs every half an hour and takes 10 minutes to reach the panoramic view of the Pyrenees and Lourdes at 3,000 feet. There is a café at the top, and it is possible to walk back down via a pathway.

Information

Open from 23 March to 11 November from 10 a.m. to 6 p.m. Adults 8 Euros return; children aged 6 to 14 years 6 Euros.

Little Train

Tour the town by train and you can alight and rejoin at any of its stopping-off points, having purchased a circular ticket. It leaves from outside St Joseph's Gate and calls at the Musée de la Nativité, the Castle Fortress, the Musée de Lourdes, the Pic du Jer Funicular Railway, the Musée Grévin and the Musée de Le Petit Lourdes.

Information

Departs every 20 minutes from 9 a.m. to 11.30 a.m. and from 1.30 p.m. to 6.15 p.m. from Palm Sunday to 31 October. From May to September departs from 8 p.m. onwards, nightly. Adults 5 Euros; children aged 6 to 12 years 2.50 Euros. Wheelchair facility.

Town Hall

The Town Hall (Mairie), The Avenue is situated in Maréchal Foch. The Town Hall in Lourdes has had five different locations, but the present imposing building, formerly known as 'Villa Roques', was built in the early twentieth century and was bought from a Madame Roques in 1942.

7

Venturing Further Afield: Places of Interest Near Lourdes

The Pyrenees form a natural frontier between France and Spain and run for 400 kilometres (250 miles) from the Atlantic Ocean to the Mediterranean Sea. It has been a popular recreational area since the early nineteenth century, with excellent climbing and walking, and more recently the development of nine ski resorts. The Parc National des Pyrénées, with free public access, covers a long narrow strip of about 100 kilometres, with a total area of 480 square kilometres (180 square miles), and in 1967 was designated as such to protect the local environment. There are clearly marked footpaths for walkers giving plenty of opportunity to see the indigenous izards (mountain goats – a Pyrenean variety of chamois) in their thousands. It provides a sanctuary for more exclusive animals and rare birds living in their natural habitat among the protected plants and wild flowers of the region.

The Department of Hautes-Pyrenees, which Lourdes comes under, is a beautiful part of the Pyrenees. With its magnificent backcloth of mountains, the highest peak being Vignemale rising to 3,298 metres (11,000 feet), plentiful rivers and lush green scenery, there is no shortage of places to visit both close to Lourdes, and a little further afield. Below are a few suggestions, but more detailed information is available from the main Tourist Office for the Pyrenees, Route de Pau, Tarbes, tel: +33 (0) 5 62 93 30 50, or from the Lourdes Tourist Office (see page 4).

BAGNÈRES-DE-BIGORRE

Bagnères-de-Bigorre is just east of Lourdes on the D938 road to Toulouse, and is a picturesque and very popular spa town and holiday resort on the River Adour. The Church of St Vincent dates from the twelfth century.

Although now quite industrialized, the centre of the town with its main square, Place Lafayette, and thermal park with hot baths, is very pleasant to visit. In August the town holds a traditional local musical festival.

A mile and a quarter away is the Grotte de Medous with fantastic stalagmites and stalactites which are reached by boat.

Information

Open July and August from 9 a.m. to 12 p.m. and from 2 p.m. to 6 p.m. From 1 April to 30 June and 1 September to 15 October open every day from 9 a.m. to 11.30 a.m. and 2 p.m. to 6 p.m. Adults 6.40 Euros; children 3.20 Euros. The visit takes one hour.

Just to the south of Bagnères-de-Bigorre, some 2,877 metres (9,500 feet) up and 50 kilometres from Lourdes, is the Pic du Midi de Bigorre Observatory. This is an exhibition area for studying the sky, sun and stars, and also gives an unrestricted view of the Pyrenees.

Information

Open from June to September from 9 a.m. to 7 p.m. Open from 1 October to 31 May from 10 a.m. to 5.30 p.m. (closed on Tuesdays during the winter). Annual closures 26 April – 30 April, and 4 November to 4 December. Adults 23 Euros; children 12 Euros.
Tel: +33 (0) 5 62 56 71 11.

BÉTHARRAM

Bétharram is situated 15 kilometres from Lourdes, off the D937 near the Bigorre border. The Grottes de Bétharram are spectacular underground caves, passing from one side of the mountain to the other through numerous caverns full of stalactites and stalagmites.

Information

Open from 25 March to 25 October from 9 a.m. to 12 p.m. and from 1.30 p.m. to 5.30 p.m. Adults 9.5 Euros; children aged 5 to 10 years 5 Euros.

BIARRITZ

Although far over on the Atlantic coast, this elegant resort made popular by the visit of Napoleon III in 1854 must be mentioned. Once a simple Basque fishing village, in the course of 100 years Biarritz has become one of the most fashionable seaside towns in France with its fine beaches, spectacular coastline, and many grand hotels and casinos. There are superb views from the Rock of the Virgin (the Rocher de la Vierge) which is linked to the maritime museum by a large aquarium.

CAUTERETS

Cauterets is at the foot of the highest peak in the Pyrenees, the Vignemale, and is a spa town dating back to Roman times. It reached the height of its popularity in the nineteenth century with many famous romantic poets such as Victor Hugo and Georges Sand visiting its waters. It is also a popular winter sports centre. From Cauterets you can continue further south on the D920, until the road comes to an end, to reach the Pont d'Espagne with its spectacular waterfalls along the way.

GAVARNIE

Gavarnie is a small village of 170 inhabitants with an interesting fourteenth-century pilgrim church. It has a long tradition of providing hospitality to merchants and pilgrims on their way to Spain. Today it welcomes tourists who come to admire one of the most natural features of the Pyrenees, the mountain amphitheatre of the Cirque de Gavarnie and the Grande Cascade, the highest waterfall in Europe with a drop of over 400 metres (1,300 feet) from which the River Gave rises.

To reach Gavarnie, take the D921 from Argelès-Gazost (13 kilometres south of Lourdes on the N21). The village is as far as you can go by vehicle, and from here it is possible to hire mules or to walk up to the all-the-year-round ice-covered Cirque de Gavarnie, with breathtaking views of the Pyrenees.

LUZ-ST-SAUVEUR

Luz-St-Sauveur halfway between Argelès-Gazost and Gavarnie on the D921, has been an important centre since the Middle Ages, with a fine twelfth-century fortified church and the castle of Saint-Marie-de-Barèges, dating back to the thirteenth century. The town is divided into two by its streams, Saint Sauveur being the side where thermal baths were constructed in 1830. In 1859 Napoleon III visited Luz-St-Sauveur with his wife Empress Eugénie, after which Pont Napoleon (Napoleon's bridge) was constructed 65 metres high over the River Gave.

ST-SAVIN

St-Savin is a picturesque village 16 kilometres from Lourdes in the Gave de Pau valley. It was once an important religious centre and the twelfth-century church and Abbey of St Savin dominate the village. St Savin was of Spanish origin, being the son of one of the Counts of Barcelona, but precise dates of his birth and death are unknown.

Nothing remains of the monastery today except the chapterhouse, some of which houses a small museum.

The church itself is in fine condition and boasts a sixteenth-century Renaissance organ, as well as wooden panels representing the life of St Savin. Unusually, the high altar of black marble is the shrine of St Savin.

The village of just over 300 inhabitants commands a wonderful view looking down over the valley, and there is an excellent café with a small gift shop. Just two kilometres on through the village you can walk up to the sixteenth-century Chapel Notre-Dame de Pietat. Sadly this is locked, but it is still worth the walk for the splendid views and peaceful surroundings.

ZOO, THE PYRENEES ANIMAL PARK

Thirteen kilometres from Lourdes at Argelès-Gazost, this park is the home of the marmot, a squirrel-like rodent that likes to be photographed! There are a variety of both large and small animals including otters, bears, izards, mouflons (wild mountain sheep), ibex and roe deer enjoying their natural environment.

Information

Open in June, July and August from 9 a.m. to 7 p.m., and from 5 April to 31 May and 1 September to 3 November from 9 a.m. to 12 p.m. and 2 p.m. to 6 p.m. Adults 8 Euros; children 6 Euros.

8

Prayers and Hymns for Pilgrims

Prayer is the focal point of every pilgrim in Lourdes, and is at the heart of our Christian faith. Whether spending a few quiet moments at the Grotto, or waiting to go into the Baths, or perhaps going round the Stations of the Cross, these familiar prayers have been chosen to help us raise our minds and hearts to God. Prayer in silence can help to concentrate the mind using a few words, *'Come Lord Jesus, Come'* and listening to what he has to say to us. In contrast, hymns give us the opportunity to praise God together, opening our hearts and voices to the glory of his name.

CHURCHES AND PLACES FOR PRIVATE PRAYER

Chapelle de la Reconciliation, Acceuil Jean-Paul II (alongside the Esplanade in the Domaine). Confessions in English are heard here from 10 a.m. to 11.15 a.m. and from 2.30 p.m. to 6 p.m.

Carmelite Chapel, 17, Rue de Pau. Although directly behind St Bernadette's Church, it is a ten-minute walk across the meadow and out through Le Porte de la Prairie (Meadow Gate) and then a right turn to reach the Chapel of this Enclosed Order (see picture in colour photo section). There is an added bonus of having a delightful view of the Domaine and the Sanctuary. It is well signposted from the Domaine.

Sisters of the Poor Clares (Monastère des Pauvres Clarisses), 78, Rue de La Grotte. The peaceful chapel in this long grey building provides a perfect haven for private prayer during a busy day in Lourdes. A nun can sometimes be seen sitting at the door concentrating on her needlework, only to be disturbed should you wish to make a purchase from the little shop inside.

Ukrainian Catholic Church, 6, Avenue Antoine Beguere. Built in 1982 and sponsored by American Ukrainians, this Byzantine church, with its gold painted domes, offers a quiet sanctuary to pilgrims a short walk on the other side of the railway line by the Rue de Pau (see picture in colour photo section). There are the traditional Russian icons, all with their own specific representations, with a theological and religious purpose using religious art as an effective means of communication.

'When you pray, do not gather up empty phrases. Your Father knows your needs before you ask him.'

Matthew 6:7–8

PRAYERS

A Prayer to Our Lady of Lourdes (Abbé Perreyve)

O Holy Virgin, in the midst of your days of glory, do not forget the sorrows of this earth. Cast a merciful glance upon those who are suffering and struggling against difficulties, with their lips constantly pressed against life's bitter cup.

Have pity on those who love each other and are separated.
Have pity on our rebellious hearts.
Have pity on our weak faith.
Have pity on those we love.
Have pity on those who weep, on those who pray, on those who fear.
Grant hope and peace to all.
Amen.

The prayer of St Francis of Assisi

Lord, make me an instrument of your peace:
Where there is hatred, let me sow love;
where there is injury, let me sow pardon;
where there is doubt, let me sow faith;
where there is despair, let me give hope;
where there is darkness, let me bring light;
where there is sadness, let me give joy.
O Divine Master, grant that I may try
not to be comforted, but to comfort;
not to be understood, but to understand;
not to be loved, but to love.
Because it is in giving that we receive;
it is in forgiving that we are forgiven,
and it in dying that we rise to eternal life.

Prayer of St Richard of Chichester

Thanks be to you, my Lord Jesus Christ, for all the benefits which you have given me; for all the pains and insults which you have borne for me. O most merciful Redeemer, Friend, and Brother, may I know you more clearly, love you more dearly, and follow you more nearly. Amen.

Dedication of all Helpers in Lourdes (Based on the Grail Prayer)

Lord Jesus, we give you our hands to do your work, and our feet to follow you.

We give you our eyes to see as you do, and our tongues to speak your words.

We give you our minds that you may think in us, and our spirit that you may pray in us.

Above all, we give you our hearts that through us you may love all mankind.

We give ourselves that you may grow in us, so that it is you Lord Jesus, who live and work and pray in us. Amen.

Cardinal Newman's Prayer for the End of the Day

May the Lord support us all the day long, till the shades lengthen and the evening comes, and the busy world is hushed, and the fever of life is over, and our work is done. Then in his mercy may he give us a safe lodging and a holy rest, and peace at the last. Amen.

Nunc Dimittis (The Song of Simeon)

Lord, now lettest thou thy servant depart in peace: according to thy word. For mine eyes have seen thy salvation, which thou hast prepared before the face of all people; to be a light to lighten the Gentiles, and to be the Glory of thy people Israel.

A Prayer for the End of our Time in Lourdes

O Mary, Mother of Jesus, we thank God, through you, for the grace of a happy pilgrimage and for all that has taken place while we have been in Lourdes. Pray for all those who have helped us, and for all our fellow pilgrims. Pray that we may have a safe and happy return home, and give us the graces to do at home what you have taught us to do here. Amen.

Our Lady of Lourdes, pray for us.
St Bernadette, pray for us.

Footprints (Margaret Fishback Powers)

One night I had a dream. I dreamed I was walking along the beach with God, and across the sky flashed scenes from my life. For each scene I noticed two sets of footprints in the sand, one belonged to me and the other to God. When the last scene of my life flashed before me I looked back at the footprints in the sand. I noticed that at times along the path of life there was only one set of footprints. I also noticed that it happened at the very lowest and saddest times of my life. This really bothered me and I questioned God about it. 'God, you said that once I decided to follow you, you would walk with me all the way, but I noticed that during the most troublesome times in my life there was only one set of footprints. I don't understand why, in times when I needed you most, you would leave me.' God replied, 'My precious, precious child, I love you and I would never, never leave you during your times of trials and suffering. When you see only one set of footprints it was then that I carried you.'

The Fatima Prayer

O my Jesus, forgive us our sins, save us from the fires of hell and lead all souls to heaven especially those who have most need of thy mercy. Amen.

THE ROSARY

The word 'rosary' is derived from a medieval custom of crowning statues of the Virgin Mary with roses. Each rose symbolized a prayer, and led to the idea of using a string of beads as a guide; in the twelfth century Cistercian monks developed this as a meditation and called it the Rosary. It is the story of the New Testament from the Annunciation to the Coronation of our Lady in heaven, following Our Lord's life. Traditionally there have been three groups reflecting the mysteries of the Gospels, but in the year 2002, the year of the Rosary, at the request of Pope John Paul II, a fourth was added, the Mysteries of Light, calling Christians to pray the rosary daily: for families and for world peace.

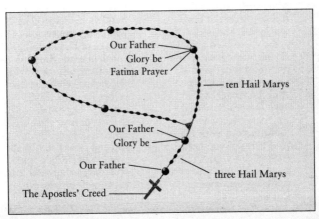

Our Father
Glory be
Fatima Prayer

ten Hail Marys

Our Father
Glory be

Our Father

three Hail Marys

The Apostles' Creed

The concept of saying the rosary is to incorporate repetitive prayer while reflecting on the life, death and resurrection of Jesus. Each group of mysteries contains five decades, which will complete one circuit of the rosary beads. You begin by reciting the Apostles' Creed, the Our Father, and three Hail Mary's, and then continue with the Our Father, Glory be to the Father, and ten Hail Marys, until the five decades have been completed. Between the praying of each decade, a mystery is brought to mind to be meditated on while praying the Rosary.

The Joyful Mysteries

1 **The Annunciation**   The Archangel Gabriel reveals to Our Lady that she has been chosen to be the mother of God's Son.

And the Angel came to Mary and said 'Hail, full of grace, the Lord is with you'. She was greatly troubled at the saying and considered in her mind what sort of greeting this might be. And the Angel said to her, 'Do not be afraid, Mary, for you have found favour with God. And behold, you will conceive in your womb and bear a son, and you shall call his name Jesus.'

Luke 1:28–31

2 **The Visitation**   Our Lady visits her cousin Elizabeth to tell her the Angel's message.

Mary rose and went with haste into the hill country, to a city of Judah, and she entered the house of Zechariah and greeted Elizabeth. And when Elizabeth heard the greeting of Mary, the babe leaped in her womb; and Elizabeth was filled with the Holy Spirit and she exclaimed with a loud cry, 'Blessed are you among women, and blessed is the fruit of your womb'.

Luke 1:39–42

3 **The Birth of Jesus**   The birth of Our Lord Jesus in a stable in Bethlehem.

And Joseph also went up from Galilee, from the city of Nazareth, to Judea, to the city of David, which is called Bethlehem, because he was of the house and lineage of David, to be enrolled with Mary his betrothed, who was with child. And while they were there, the time came for her to be delivered. And she gave birth to her first-born son and wrapped him in swaddling clothes, and laid him in a manger because there was no place for them in the inn.

Luke 2:4–7

4 **The Presentation** Our Lord is presented in the Temple in Jerusalem as was the custom of the Jews.

> And when the time came for their purification according to the law of Moses, they brought him up to Jerusalem to present him to the Lord, and to offer a sacrifice according to what is said in the law of the Lord, 'a pair of turtle-doves or two young pigeons'.
>
> Luke 2:22, 24

5 **Finding of the Child Jesus in the Temple** Mary and Joseph find Jesus in the Temple when he is 12 years old, going about his Father's business.

> After three days they found Jesus in the temple, sitting among the teachers, listening to them and asking them questions; and all who heard him were amazed at his understanding and his answers. And when Mary and Joseph saw him they were astonished; and his mother said to him, 'Son, why have you treated us so? Behold, your father and I have been looking for you anxiously.' And he said to them, 'How is it that you sought me? Did you not know that I must be in my Father's house?'
>
> Luke 2:46–49

The Sorrowful Mysteries

1 **The Agony in the Garden** Jesus goes to the Garden of Gethsamene to pray for strength to bear his Passion and he sweated blood.

> And being in an agony he prayed more earnestly; and his sweat became like great drops of blood falling down upon the ground. And when he rose from prayer, he came to the disciples and found them sleeping for sorrow, and he said to them, 'Why do you sleep? Rise and pray that you may not enter into temptation.'
>
> Luke 22:44–46

2 **The Scourging at the Pillar** Jesus is flogged before Pilate.

> Then Pilate released for them Barabbas, and having scourged Jesus, delivered him to be crucified.
>
> Matthew 27:26

3 **The Crowning with Thorns** Jesus is stripped of his clothes and a crown of thorns is placed on his head. The crowd shout out, 'Hail, King of the Jesus!'

> And the soldiers stripped him and put a

67

scarlet robe upon him, and plaiting a crown of thorns they put it on his head, and put a reed in his right hand. And kneeling before him they mocked him, saying, 'Hail, King of the Jews!' And they spat upon him, and took the reed and struck him on the head. And when they had mocked him, they stripped him of the robe, and put his own clothes on him, and led him away to crucify him.

Matthew 27:28–31

4 **The Carrying of the Cross** Our Blessed Lord carries his cross towards the place called the Skull, which in Hebrew is Golgotha.

So they took Jesus, and he went out, bearing his own cross, to the place called the Place of the Skull, which is called in Hebrew, Golgotha.

John 19:17

5 **The Crucifixion** Jesus dies on the cross and puts his trust into his Father's hands. 'Father, into thy hands I commit my spirit!'

It was now about the sixth hour, and there was darkness over the whole land until the ninth hour, while the sun's light failed; and the curtain of the temple was torn in two. Then Jesus, crying with a loud voice, said, 'Father, into thy hands I commit my spirit!' And having said this he breathed his last.

Luke 23:44–46

The Glorious Mysteries

1 **The Resurrection** Jesus rises from the dead – the stone has been moved and his tomb is empty.

And very early on the first day of the week Mary Magdalene, Mary the mother of James, and Salome went to the tomb when the sun had risen. And they were saying to one another, 'Who will roll away the stone for us from the door of the tomb?' And looking up, they saw that the stone was rolled back; for it was very large. And entering the tomb, they saw a young man sitting on the right side, dressed in a white robe; and they were amazed. And he said to them, 'Do not be amazed; you seek Jesus of Nazarath, who was crucified. He has risen, he is not here; see the place where they laid him.'

Mark 16:2–6

2 **The Ascension** Our Lord ascends into heaven, and sits on the right hand of God.

So when they had come together, the Apostles asked him, 'Lord, will you at this time restore the kingdom to Israel?' He said to them, 'It is not for you to know times or seasons which the Father has fixed by his own authority. But you shall receive power when the Holy Spirit has come upon you; and you shall be my witnesses in Jerusalem and in all Judea and Samaria and to the end of the Earth.' And when he had said this, as they were looking on, he was lifted up, and a cloud took him out of their sight.

Acts 1:6–9

3 **The Descent of the Holy Spirit** The power of the Holy Spirit comes down from heaven, and all heard in their own tongue the wonderful works of God.

When the day of Pentecost had come, the Apostles were all together in one place. And suddenly a sound came from heaven like the rush of a mighty wind, and it filled all the house where they were sitting. And there appeared to them tongues as of fire, distributed and resting on each one of them. And they were all filled with the Holy Spirit and began to speak in other tongues, as the Spirit gave them utterance.

Acts 2:1–4

4 **The Assumption** Our Blessed Lady is taken up body and soul into Heaven.

And a great portent appeared in heaven, a woman clothed with the sun, with the moon under her feet, and on her head a crown of twelve stars.

Revelation 12:1

5 **The Coronation** Our Blessed Lady is crowned Queen of Heaven amid the glory of all the Saints.

They all blessed her with one accord and said to her, 'You are the exaltation of Jerusalem, you are the great glory of Israel, you are the great pride of our nation . . . May the almighty Lord bless you forever.'

Judith 15:9–10

The Mysteries of Light

1 **Christ's Baptism in the Jordan** John the Baptist baptizes Jesus in the River Jordan

In those days Jesus came from Nazareth of Galilee and was baptized by John in the Jordan. And when he came up out of the water, immediately he saw the heavens opened and the Spirit descending upon him like a dove; and a voice came from heaven,

69

'Thou art my beloved Son; with thee I am well pleased.'

Mark 1:9–11

2 Christ's Self-Revelation at the Marriage at Cana The first Miracle when Jesus changes water into wine at the Wedding Feast

On the third day there was a marriage at Cana in Galilee, and the mother of Jesus was there; Jesus also was invited to the marriage with his disciples. When the wine failed, the mother of Jesus said to him, 'They have no wine.' . . . Now six stone jars were standing there for the Jewish rites of purification, each holding twenty or thirty gallons. Jesus said to them, 'Fill the jars with water.' And they filled them up to the brim. He said to them, 'Now draw some out and take it to the steward of the feast.' So they took it. When the steward of the feast tasted the water now become wine, and did not know where it came from, the steward called the bridegroom and said to him, 'Every man serves the good wine first; and when men have drunk freely, then the poor wine; but you have kept the good wine until now.' This,

the first of his signs, Jesus did at Cana in Galilee, and manifested his glory; and his disciples believed in him.

John 2:1–3, 6

3 Christ's Proclamation of the Kingdom of God with his Call to Conversion Jesus asks for repentance and belief in the good news that the Kingdom of God is nigh.

Now after John was arrested, Jesus came into Galilee, preaching the gospel of God and saying, 'The time is fulfilled, and the kingdom of God is at hand; repent, and believe in the gospel.'

Mark 1:14–15

4 Christ's Transfiguration The mystical and visionary occurrence on Mount Hermon in which the spirit which possessed Jesus became visible to three of the disciples.

After six days Jesus took with him Peter and James and John his brother, and led them up a high mountain apart. And he was transfigured before them, and his face shone like the sun, and his garments became white as light.

Matthew 17:1–2

5 **Christ's Institution of the Eucharist** Jesus takes Bread, gives it to his disciples saying, 'This is my body, which is given for you. Do this in remembrance of me.'

And he took bread, and when he had given thanks he broke it and gave it to them, saying, 'This is my body which is given for you. Do this in remembrance of me.' And likewise the cup after supper, saying, 'This cup which is poured out for you is the new covenant in my blood.'

Luke 22:19-20

Hail Mary, full of grace, the Lord is with thee; blessed art thou among women, and blessed is the fruit of thy womb, Jesus. Holy Mary, mother of God, pray for us sinners, now and at the hour of our death. Amen.

Pray for us, O Holy Mother of God, That we may be made worthy of the promises of Christ.

STATIONS OF THE CROSS

First Station: Jesus is Condemned to Death

Then Pilate saw that he was making no impression, that in fact a riot was imminent. So he took some water, washed his hands in front of the crowd saying, 'I am innocent of this man's blood; see to it yourselves'. Then the people as a whole answered, 'His blood be on us and on our children!' So he released Barabbas for them; and after flogging Jesus, he handed him over to be crucified.

Matthew 27:24-26

Leader: We adore you, O Christ, and we praise you;
Response: **Because by your holy cross you have redeemed the world.**
Reflection: Pilate has just passed the death sentence on an innocent man out of fear of the reaction of the crowds. Dear Lord, give us strength to do what is right, despite what other people around us may think.

I love you, Jesus my love, above all things; I repent with all my heart for having offended you. Never permit me to separate myself from you again. Grant that I may always love you, and then do with me whatever you wish.

At the Cross her station keeping
Stood the mournful Mother weeping,
Close to Jesus to the last.

71

Second Station: Jesus Takes up his Cross

So they took Jesus; and carrying the cross by himself, he went out to what is called the Place of the Skull, which in Hebrew is called Golgotha.

John 19:16–17

Leader: We adore you, O Christ, and we praise you;
Response: **Because by your holy cross you have redeemed the world.**
Reflection: Jesus willingly accepts the cross for all our sakes. Help us, Lord, to accept our own burdens in this life with the same love that you showed for us.

I love you, Jesus, my love, above all things; I repent with all my heart for having offended you. Never permit me to separate myself from you again. Grant that I may always love you, and then do with me whatever you wish.

Through her heart, his
sorrow sharing,
All his bitter anguish
bearing,
Now at length the sword has
passed.

Third Station: Jesus Falls for the First Time

Yet ours were the sufferings he was bearing, ours the sorrows he was carrying, while we thought

of him as someone being punished and struck with affliction by God; whereas he was being wounded for our rebellions, crushed because of our guilt; the punishment reconciling us fell on him, and we have been healed by his bruises.

Isaiah 53:4–5

Leader: We adore you O Christ, and we praise you;
Response: **Because by your holy cross you have redeemed the world.**
Reflection: It is human weakness that brings Jesus to his knees, and yet he gets up on his feet to struggle on to Calvary. When our human weaknesses make us stumble, Lord, give us the strength to rise to our feet again.

I love you, Jesus, my love, above all things; I repent with all my heart for having offended you. Never permit me to separate myself from you again. Grant that I may always love you, and then do with me whatever you wish.

Oh, how sad and sore
distressed
Was that Mother highly blest
Of the sole-begotten One.

Fourth Station: Jesus Meets his Mother, Mary

Simeon blessed them and said to Mary his mother, 'You see this child: he is destined for the fall and for the rising of many in Israel, destined to be a sign that is rejected – and a sword will pierce your own soul too – so that the secret thoughts of many may be laid bare.'

Luke 2:34–35

Leader: We adore you O Christ, and we praise you;

Response: **Because by your holy cross you have redeemed the world.**

Reflection: Mary shares her son's suffering, but both give strength to each other through their mutual love. May we too offer that same love and support to others who are having difficult times.

I love you, Jesus, my love, above all things; I repent with all my heart for having offended you. Never permit me to separate myself from you again. Grant that I may always love you, and then do with me whatever you wish.

Is there one who would not weep,
Overwhelmed in miseries deep
Christ's dear Mother to behold?

Fifth Station: Simon of Cyrene Helps Jesus to Carry his Cross

As they were leading him away they seized on a man, Simon from Cyrene, who was coming in from the country, and made him shoulder the cross and carry it behind Jesus.

Luke 23:26

Leader: We adore you O Christ, and we praise you;

Response: **Because by your holy cross you have redeemed the world.**

Reflection: Simon must have found it difficult being picked from the huge crowd to be the one to help Jesus shoulder the cross. We too must be willing to help as apostles in the world by giving service to others both by deed and by example.

I love you, Jesus, my love, above all things; I repent with all my heart for having offended you. Never permit me to separate myself from you again. Grant that I may always love you, and then do with me whatever you wish.

Can the human heart refrain
From partaking in her pain,
Is that Mother's pain untold?

Sixth Station: Veronica Wipes the Face of Jesus

Like a sapling he grew up before him, like a root in arid ground. He had no form or charm to attract us, no beauty to win our hearts; he was despised, the lowest of men, a man of sorrows, familiar with suffering, one from whom, as it were, we averted our gaze, despised, for whom we had no regard. Yet

73

ours were the sufferings he was bearing, ours the sorrows he was carrying . . .

Isaiah 53:2–4

Leader: We adore you O Christ, and we praise you;

Response: **Because by your holy cross you have redeemed the world.**

Reflection: Veronica breaks through the crowd to bring Jesus a little relief by refreshingly wiping his face. She did not hesitate to come to his aid, despite the possible consequences of her action. Help us to be the Good Samaritan, and not hang back when we are needed.

I love you, Jesus, my love, above all things; I repent with all my heart for having offended you. Never permit me to separate myself from you again. Grant that I may always love you, and then do with me whatever you wish.

Bruised, derided, cursed, defiled,
She beheld her tender Child
All with bloody scourges rent.

Seventh Station: Jesus Falls for the Second Time

Now that I have fallen, they crowd round delighted,
flocking to jeer at me;
strangers I never even knew
with loud cries to tear me to pieces,

riddling me with jibe after jibe,
grinding their teeth at me.

Psalm 35:15–16

Leader: We adore you O Christ, and we praise you;

Response: **Because by your holy cross you have redeemed the world.**

Reflection: Jesus is carrying the burden of our sins, and at every step his path gets harder until he falls for a second time. However many times we fall during our pilgrimage of life, Jesus is there to help us when we stand up once more.

I love you, Jesus, my love, above all things; I repent with all my heart for having offended you. Never permit me to separate myself from you again. Grant that I may always love you, and then do with me whatever you wish.

O thou Mother! Fount of love!
Touch my spirit from above,
Make my heart with thine accord.

Eighth Station: Jesus Consoles the Women of Jerusalem

Large numbers of people followed him, and of women too, who mourned and lamented for him. But Jesus turned to them and said, 'Daughters of Jerusalem, do not weep for me; weep rather for

74

yourselves and for your children.'

Luke 23:27–28

Leader: We adore you O Christ, and we praise you;
Response: **Because by your holy cross you have redeemed the world.**
Reflection: Despite his pain and anguish, Jesus turns to the women of Jerusalem telling them that they are to be pitied more than he is, and not to weep for him. He asks them to recognize what is really happening, and to look to the future. We as his children must have the spirit to keep our faith alive in the Church today.

I love you, Jesus, my love, above all things; I repent with all my heart for having offended you. Never permit me to separate myself from you again. Grant that I may always love you, and then do with me whatever you wish.

Make me feel as thou hast felt;
Make my soul to glow and melt
With the love of Christ my Lord.

Ninth Station: Jesus Falls for the Third Time

But he emptied himself taking the form of a slave, becoming as human beings are; and being in every way like a human being, he was humbler yet, even

to accepting death, death on a cross.

Philippians 2:7–8

Leader: We adore you O Christ, and we praise you;
Response: **Because by your holy cross you have redeemed the world.**
Reflection: It would seem that this really is the end of the journey: Jesus is now alone because the soldiers have pushed back the crowds. Lord, help us to remember how you carried our sins on your cross and thereby keep in our minds our Christian duty before our own selfish needs.

I love you, Jesus, my love, above all things; I repent with all my heart for having offended you. Never permit me to separate myself from you again. Grant that I may always love you, and then do with me whatever you wish.

Let me mingle tears with thee,
Mourning him who mourned for me,
All the days that I may live.

Tenth Station: Jesus is Stripped of his Garments

When the soldiers had finished crucifying Jesus they took his clothing and divided it into four shares, one for each soldier. His undergarment was seamless, woven in one piece from neck to hem; so they said to one another, 'Instead of tearing it, let's throw dice to decide who is to have it.' In this way the words of the scripture were fulfilled: *They shared out my garments among them. They cast lots for my clothes.* This is exactly what the soldiers did.

John 19:23–24

Leader: We adore you O Christ, and we praise you;
Response: **Because by your holy cross you have redeemed the world.**
Reflection: Jesus stands humiliated in public, all sense of dignity having been removed. His clothes have been discarded to be shared out between the soldiers. They have even cast lots. Let us reflect on his suffering and strip ourselves of all that is unhealthy in our lives, keeping our minds on all that is good.

I love you, Jesus, my love, above all things; I repent with all my heart for having offended you. Never permit me to separate myself from you again. Grant that I may always love you, and then do with me whatever you wish.

Let me share with thee
his pain
Who for all my sins was
slain,
Who for me in torments
died.

Eleventh Station: Jesus is Nailed to the Cross

When they reached the place called The Skull, there they crucified him and the two criminals, one on his right, the other on his left. Jesus said, 'Father forgive them; they do not know what they are doing.' Then they cast lots to share out his clothing.

Luke 23:33–34

Leader: We adore you O Christ, and we praise you;
Response: **Because by your holy cross you have redeemed the world.**
Reflection: Until this time the cross had been a symbol of shame and failure, but has since become a sign of love and hope. As Jesus was nailed to the cross between two criminals he asked his Father to forgive his crucifiers as they did not know what they were doing. Lord, give us the grace by your example to forgive others as you forgive us.

I love you, Jesus, my love, above all things; I repent with all my heart for having offended you. Never permit me to separate myself from you again. Grant that I may always love you, and then do with me whatever you wish.

Christ above in torment
hangs;
She beneath beholds the
pangs
Of her dying glorious Son.

Twelfth Station: Jesus Dies on the Cross

It was now about the sixth
hour and, with the sun
eclipsed, a darkness came
over the whole land until
the ninth hour. The veil of
the temple was torn right
down the middle; and,
when Jesus had cried out
in a loud voice, he said,
*'Father, into your hands I
commend my spirit.'* With
these words he breathed
his last.

Luke 23:44–46

Leader: We adore you O
Christ, and we praise you;
Response: **Because by your
holy cross you have
redeemed the world.**
Reflection: Jesus had made
the ultimate sacrifice. He
had given up his life to
save sinners even though
he was challenged by the
soldiers to save himself if
he truly was the Son of
God. He had done his
Father's will. Teach us to
trust in God's will and
when our time comes to
commend our spirit into
his hands.

I love you, Jesus, my love,
above all things; I repent
with all my heart for having
offended you. Never permit
me to separate myself from

you again. Grant that I may
always love you, and then do
with me whatever you wish.

Holy Mother, pierce me
through;
In my heart each wound
renew
Of my Saviour crucified.

Thirteenth Station: Jesus is Taken Down from the Cross

After this, Joseph of
Arimathaea, who was a
disciple of Jesus – though
a secret one because he
was afraid of the Jews –
asked Pilate to let him
remove the body of Jesus.
Pilate gave permission, so
they came and took it
away. Nicodemus came as
well – the same one who
had first come to Jesus at
night-time – and he
brought a mixture of
myrrh and aloes, weighing
several pounds.

John 19:38–39

Leader: We adore you O
Christ, and we praise you;
Response: **Because by your
holy cross you have
redeemed the world.**
Reflection: It is now that we
can reflect on the death of
Christ, and what it must
have meant to his
bewildered mother Mary
to hold the lifeless body of
her beloved son. Lord,
give strength to all of
those who suffer the
tragedy of losing a child,

77

and help them in their grief. It is our belief that by dying Jesus destroyed our death, giving us the only complete meaning to our lives.

I love you, Jesus, my love, above all things; I repent with all my heart for having offended you. Never permit me to separate myself from you again. Grant that I may always love you, and then do with me whatever you wish.

Christ, when thou shalt call
me hence,
Be they Mother my defence,
Be thy Cross my victory.

Fourteenth Station: Jesus is Laid in the Tomb

They took the body of Jesus and wrapped it with the spices in linen clothes, following the Jewish burial custom. At the place where he had been crucified there was a garden, and in this garden a new tomb in which no one had yet been buried. Since it was the Jewish day of Preparation and the tomb was near at hand, they laid Jesus there.
John 19:40–42

Leader: We adore you O Christ, and we praise you;
Response: **Because by your holy cross you have redeemed the world**
Reflection: Jesus has come to the end of his journey, and now having been placed in

a silent tomb his work on earth is finished. In following the Way of the Cross we have shared in the suffering of Christ. Lord, help us to take up our cross in order that we should not be dragged down by our daily struggles.

I love you, Jesus, my love, above all things; I repent with all my heart for having offended you. Never permit me to separate myself from you again. Grant that I may always love you, and then do with me whatever you wish.

While my body here decays,
May my soul thy goodness
praise,
Safe in Paradise with thee.

Fifteenth Station: The Resurrection

On the first day of the week, at the first sign of dawn, they went to the tomb with the spices they had prepared. They found the stone had been rolled away from the tomb but on entering discovered that the body of the Lord Jesus was not there.
Luke 24:1–3

Rising you restored our life

'He is not here; he has risen.'

The stone in front of the tomb has been rolled to one side; the body of

Jesus has gone. We stand and reflect on the true meaning of his Passion and death.

This fifteenth station has been added as a reminder of what took place the morning after the Crucifixion.

HYMNS

Lourdes Hymn: Ave Maria

1. Immaculate Mary!
   Our hearts are on fire,
   that title so wondrous
   fills all our desire,

   Ave, ave, ave Maria!
   Ave, ave, ave Maria!

2. We pray for God's
      glory,
   may his kingdom come!
   We pray for his vicar,
   our Father, and Rome.

3. We pray for our mother
   the church upon earth,
   and bless, sweetest
      Lady,
   the land of our birth.

4. For poor, sick, afflicted
   thy mercy we crave;
   and comfort the dying,
   thou light of the grave.

5. There is no need, Mary,
   nor ever has been
   which thou canst not
      succour,
   Immaculate Queen.

6. In grief and temptation,
   in joy or in pain,
   we'll ask thee, our
      mother,
   nor seek thee in vain.

7. O bless us, dear Lady,
   with blessings from
      heaven,
   and to our petitions
   let answer be given.

8. In death's solemn
      moment,
   our mother, be nigh;
   as children of Mary
   O teach us to die.

9. And crown thy sweet
      mercy
   with this special grace,
   to behold soon in
      heaven
   God's ravishing face.

10. Now to God be all glory
    and worship for aye,
    and to God's virgin
       mother
    an endless Ave.

              Author unknown

Salve, Regina

Salve, Regina, Mater
misericordiae;
Vita, dulcedo et spes nostra,
salve.
Ad te clamamus, exsules filii
Hevae.
Ad te suspiramus gementes
et flentes
in hac lacrimarum valle.
Eia ergo advocata nostra,
illos tuos
misericordes oculos, ad nos
converte.
Et Jesum, benedictum
fructum ventris
tui, nobis post hoc exsilium
ostende.
O Clemens, O pia,
O dulcis Virgo Maria.

Hail, holy Queen, mother of
mercy;
Hail, our life, our sweetness
and our hope!
To thee do we cry, poor
banished children of
Eve; to thee do we send up
our sighs
mourning and weeping in
this vale of tears.
Turn then most gracious
advocate thine eyes
of mercy towards us; and
after this our exile,
show unto us the blessed
fruit of thy womb, Jesus.
O clement, O loving,
O sweet Virgin Mary

Traditional anthem

1. As I kneel before you,
   as I bow my head in
       prayer,
   take this day, make it
       yours
   and fill me with your
       love.

   Ave, Maria, gratia plena,
   Dominus tecum,
       beneticta tu.

2. All I have I give you,
   ev'ry dream and wish are
       yours.
   Mother of Christ, Mother
       of mine,
   present them to my
       Lord.

3. As I kneel before you,
   and I see your smiling
       face,
   ev'ry thought, ev'ry
       word
   is lost in your embrace.

   Maria Parkinson

1. Amazing grace! How
      sweet the sound
   that saved a wretch like
      me.
   I once was lost, but now
      I'm found,
   was blind, and now I
      see.

2. 'Twas grace that taught
      my heart to fear,
   and grace my fears
      relieved.
   How precious did that
      grace appear
   the hour I first believed.

3. Through many dangers,
      toils and snares
   I have already come.
   'Tis grace hath brought
      me safe thus far,
   and grace will lead me
      home.

4. The Lord has promised
      good to me;
   his word my hope
      secures.
   He will my shield and
      portion be
   as long as life endures.
                John Newton
                (1725–1807)

1. He who would
      valiant be
   'gainst all disaster,
   let him in constancy
   follow the Master.
   There's no
      discouragement
   shall make him once
      relent
   his first avowed intent
   to be a pilgrim.

2. Who so beset him round
   with dismal stories,
   do but themselves
      confound –
   his strength the more is.
   No foes shall stay his
      might,
   though he with giants
      fight:
   he will make good his
      right
   to be a pilgrim.

3. Since, Lord, thou dost
      defend
   us with thy Spirit,
   we know we at the end
   shall life inherit.
   Then fancies flee away!
   I'll fear not what men
      say,
   I'll labour night and day
   to be a Pilgrim.
    Percy Dearmer (1867–1936)
    after John Bunyan (1628–88)

Glossary

Accueil 'Welcome', the prefix given to the hospitals for the sick in Lourdes.

Addison's Disease A condition associated with a deficiency of adrenal corticosteroids, characterized by weakness, low blood pressure and pigmentation of the skin (see miracles).

amphitheatre A roofed or unroofed area with tiered seating around a central space.

apparition An unexpected or sudden appearance (see page 14).

authenticate To establish as worthy of belief.

'Ave Maria' The Lourdes Hymn (see page 79).

Basilica A church based on an ancient Roman Public Hall.

Basques Natives of the Western Pyrenees (see page 7).

Benediction A blessing at the end of a service, particularly the Blessed Sacrament Procession.

Blessed Sacrament Procession A procession with the sacramental presence of Jesus in the form of bread and wine (see page 37).

Brancardiers and Handmaids men and women who help to care for the sick in Lourdes.

bratelles Leather or canvas straps worn by Brancardiers.

cachot A dungeon or prison cell (see page 38).

Calvary The place where Christ was crucified.

canonization The declaration that a deceased person becomes a saint.

Catechism The principles of religion in the form of questions and answers.

ciborium A drinking cup or chalice. The chalice used by Our Lord at the Last Supper is known as the Holy Grail.

Cistercian Order A stricter branch of the Benedictines founded in 1098.

Cité Secours St Pierre The City of the Poor (see page 39).

couchette A sleeping berth on a train.

Credo The Nicene Creed is one of the fundamental statements of Christianity, promulagated by the

Council of Nicea in 325 AD.

crozier A hooked staff carried by a bishop, symbolizing a shepherd's crook.

crypt An underground vault beneath a church (see page 45).

diorama A small representation of scenes consisting of three-dimensional figures (see page 53).

dogma a principle as laid down by the authority of a church.

Domaine The area encompassing the Shrines in Lourdes (see page 40).

en trinquet An indoor version of the Basque game *pelota* (see page 7).

esplanade A level open space for walking along, often by the seaside.

Euskaldunak, Euskadi and Euskara The people, country and language of the Basques (see page 7).

Extreme Unction The last rites in the Roman Catholic Church, administered when the penitent is seriously ill or at the point of death (see page 19).

Feast of the Annunciation The announcement of the incarnation of Jesus made by the Archangel Gabriel to Mary, commemorated on Lady Day, 25 March.

Feast of the Immaculate Conception The doctrine that the Virgin Mary was free from original sin from the moment of her conception, commemorated on 8 December.

Franciscan A friar or nun of the Religions Order founded by St Francis of Assisi in 1209.

Fronton A high wall adjoining the pitch on which is played the Basque game, pelota (see page 7).

funicular A cable railway, used especially on a mountainside (see page 56).

grotto A small picturesque cave (see page 41).

Greek Cross A cross with four equal arms (see Rosary Basilica, page 47).

Hemicycle A semi-circular figure or building (see page 43).

Hodgkin's Disease A malignant disease of the lymph nodes named after an English physician, Thomas Hodgkin (1798–1866) (see miracles).

hospice A home for people who are ill or who need to rest or recuperate, especially one run by a religious order (see page 55).

Izarra A green or yellow Pyrenean liqueur (see page 8).

Lamb of God Agnus Dei – Jesus Christ.

last rites Sacred acts for a person just before death or when they are very ill.

Mairie Town Hall.

Marian devotion Relating to the Virgin Mary (see Crowned Virgin, page 40).

Maundy Thursday The day before Good Friday in Holy Week commemorating the Last Supper.

monstrance A vessel in which the Host is exposed for veneration.

mosaic A pattern produced by an arrangement of small variously coloured pieces of stone (or glass).

Neo-Byzantine In the style of the Eastern Roman Empire (see Rosary Basilica, page 47).

novena A devotion of special prayers on nine successive days (see miracles).

novitiate A period of time served by a novice joining a Religious Order.

pelota A popular local Basque sport (see page 7).

peritonitis Inflammation of the membrane that lines the abdominal cavity (see miracles).

petition a solemn prayer, often written.

Place ou Priait Place of prayer (see Grotto, page 41).

Piscines The Baths where pilgrims bathe in the Lourdes water (see page 36).

Pont Vieux Old Bridge. The old bridge in Lourdes, which connects the new town with the old town, dates back to Roman times.

portico A roof supported by columns at regular intervals (see Underground Basilica, page 48).

Pott's Disease Tuberculosis of the spine caused by drinking infected cow's milk, named after an English surgeon, Sir Percivall Pott (1713–88) (see miracles).

prairie A meadow.

rampart A walkway on a defensive wall.

rebot A five-team version of the Basque game, *pelota*.

reliquary A receptacle for relics such as a coffin or a shrine.

Renaissance The revival of art in the classical style.

Romanesque Style of architecture with massive vaulting and round arches, between 900 and 1200.

Rosary A form of devotion or a string of 55 beads (from the Saxon *biddan* meaning to pray), for keeping count of the five decades of the Rosary prayers (see page 65).

Salus Infirmorum A fine monument in the Domaine erected by the Diocese of Cambrai in 1912 (see page 45).

'Salve, Regina' 'Hail (holy) Queen', a popular Marian antiphon, sung or said after compline in the evening (see page 80).

sanctuary A holy place.

sarcophagus A stone coffin, usually with an inscription.

Scala Sancta Holy steps, the first Station of the Cross where some pilgrims climb the steps on their knees as an act of penance.

shrine A chapel, church or altar sacred to a saint.

Stagier A voluntary helper.

tableau A group of people forming a picturesque scene.

Tome de Brebis A local Basque cheese.

Torchlight Procession The evening procession round the Esplanade congregating in Rosary Square (see page 49).

Trappist Monk A member of an austere Cistercian Order founded in 1124 in Normandy.

triptych A picture or relief carving made up of three panels hinged together (see Bartrès Church, page 52).

tuberculosis A widespread disease of the nineteenth century characterized by the formation of nodular lesions (see miracles).

tympanum A carving in a space over a door between the lintel and the arch.

voiture A three-wheeled carriage with a hood, used for pulling pilgrims (see page 50).

votive stand A stand for placing a candle as a prayer for your special intentions. In Lourdes there are different sized votive stands to accommodate all sizes of candles which burn throughout the day and night.

Way of the Cross The 15 Stations of the Cross which follow the passion, death and resurrection of Christ (see pages 50, 71).

Index